Apple intends to donate its portion of the proceeds derived from this book to the International Society for Technology and Education (ISTE). ISTE is a membership organization for technology-using educators, dedicated to promoting appropriate uses of technology to support and improve learning, teaching, and administration.

Computers
in the
Classroom

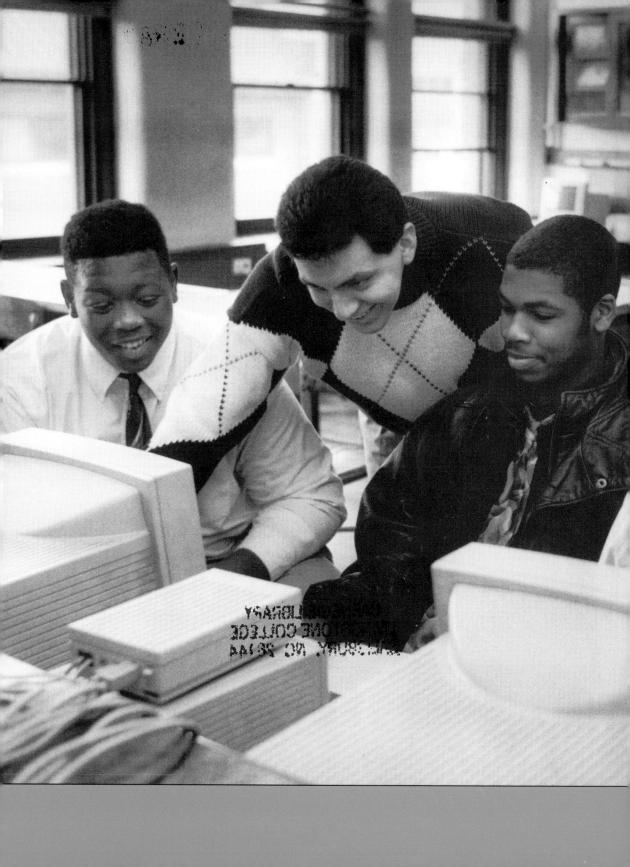

Computers
in the
Classroom

How Teachers and Students Are Using Technology to Transform Learning

Andrea R. Gooden
Fred Silverman, Editor
Julie Chase, Photographer

Apple
PRESS

A Jossey-Bass and
Apple Press Publication

This book can be ordered from Jossey-Bass Inc., Publishers at 1-800-956-7739.

For sales outside the United States, please contact your local Simon & Schuster International Office.

Substantial discounts on bulk quantities of Jossey-Bass books are available to corporations, professional associations, and other organizations. For details and discount information, contact the special sales department at Jossey-Bass Inc., Publishers (415) 433-1740; Fax (800) 605-2665.

Cover Photograph by Julie Chase

Text design by Paula Goldstein

Manufactured in the United States of America.

Library of Congress Cataloging-in-Publication Data
Gooden, Andrea R.
    Computers in the classroom: how teachers and students are using
technology to transform learning / Andrea R. Gooden; Fred
Silverman, editor; Julie Chase, photographer. — 1st ed.
ISBN 0-7879-0262-4
    p.   cm.
    Includes index.
    1. Computer-assisted instruction—United States—Case studies.
2. Educational technology—United States—Case studies.   3. School
improvement programs—United States—Case studies.   I. Silverman,
Fred, date.   II. Title.
LB1028.43.G65 1996
371.3'34'0973—dc20   96-25206
                                                                            CIP
FIRST EDITION
HB Printing   10 9 8 7 6 5 4 3 2 1

Contents

Foreword

The Need for School Reform

Educators and the general public alike are well aware that there are many new demands upon schools, both public and private, arising from major social and economic transformations that require new skills and approaches to learning. These changes range widely:

- The redefinition of work based on the development of technology and the internationalization of trade
- The growth of cultural diversity
- The increasing need for effective services for the poor and disenfranchised
- The demand for solutions to problems created by the dissolution of civic sensibility and community life

These changes imply new educational strategies and, if necessary, fundamental alteration in the way schools work.

Educational reformers advocate changes that promise solutions to some of these problems:

- Developing sophisticated thinking skills and the ability to think in an integrated and holistic manner that crosses traditional subject area boundaries
- Integrating cultural diversity into pedagogical practice (instead of excluding it, at the cost of losing a high percentage of the students)
- Providing learning that crosses traditional curricular boundaries and involves and excites students (rather than boring them or making them actively hostile to school)
- Reconnecting the school to the community it serves, to utilize community resources in school learning and to see students as valuable and integral members of the community (rather than as hostile intruders on the polity)
- Connecting school to the actual world the students will live and work in for the rest of their lives
- Perhaps most important of all, inspiring students with hope in their own and the world's future and manifesting their valued place in the community and society

Even assuming an acknowledgment of the need to change and the plausibility of the solutions, it is very difficult for institutions to reform themselves. Public schools in particular have been resistant to change over the years, although currently they face the choice of reforming or dying away. Critiques of public schools are not new, nor are major social transformations within our society. As far back as the end of the nineteenth century, the nature of public education was reexamined in light of massive integration of Italian, Irish, and Eastern European newcomers. There was a cry to broaden education to prepare rural peasant immigrant workers for life in the city and work in the factory. Teaching English and citizenship were major concerns.

It was during the early twentieth century, as a consequence of these new demands on schooling, that the high school as we presently know it was created. Fifty-minute periods, lockers in the hall, and the departmental division of subject matter were developed along the model of the school as an industrial factory. These innovations are less than a century old, though to some they may seem eternal and fixed forms of schooling.

At about the same time, student-centered education oriented toward the students' experience and community-based learning developed, largely through the work of John Dewey and the Progressive Education Association. This came into direct conflict with the tradition of didactic, teacher-centered education derived from early church schools. The opposition between these two ways of organizing schooling is fundamentally over the questions of how democratic citizenship is best instilled in the young and how creativity and ingenuity are best fostered in children.

This latter problem became central during the 1950s as a result of the shock of *Sputnik*. The Kennedy administration mobilized scientists and educators to examine the public schools and develop new curriculum materials and pedagogical techniques that would enable the United States to resume its lead in creative and innovative science. This led to the development of the New Science and New Math programs. Unfortunately, these programs were created by university-based scientists and educational specialists; they lost a great deal in translation into everyday classroom practice. Lacking the cooperation and insight of classroom practitioners, the new approaches were too remote from the realities of working with large groups of children. Teachers simply did not use them.

One of the things innovators learned from these ventures was that if you are to change the schools, then practicing, experienced teachers must be involved at the beginning and throughout the process of innovation. And you have to provide classroom teachers with models of good teaching as well as the time to grow into new ways of teaching. This implies reforming teacher education, developing model schools where teachers can be exposed to good practice, and creating supportive administrations that encourage teachers to be innovative.

A major reform issue has been the education of the underserved in our nation. Although physical desegregation of public schools is no longer a burning issue, the problem of creating quality public education for minority students persists, especially with the recent influx of new immigrants.

In fact, demographic changes have influenced the entire educational system. The development of multicultural education has led to revision of textbooks, a broadening of the ways in which classrooms are organized, and controversies over who can best teach children of color. It has also stirred up major cultural conflicts over whether the dominant European American culture should be the exclusively sanctioned cultural mode for the schools. Thus, issues of curriculum reform; the teaching of contemporary mathematics and sciences; the mainstreaming of students with disabilities; and the specifics of school district, school, and classroom organization are framed in the context of current cultural wars that have spilled over from the schools and universities into the political arena. Consequently, school reform is also on the cutting edge of political debates over what America is to be as a society.

Current critics of public education come from all strands of the political spectrum and do not share a common educational philosophy. What they agree on, however, is that student achievement is substandard, the curriculum is out of date, and the social organization of school is inadequate to deal with the moral, economic, intellectual, and social problems young people face.

Enter the Computer

All of these problems, whose historical roots can be traced to the beginnings of our society, have to be reconsidered in the light of other, revolutionary components of education: computing, electronic communications, cyberspace worlds. When I began teaching in 1962, computers belonged to the corporate and military worlds. It was unthinkable that in the span of my teaching career there would be multiple computers in every kindergarten, that the classroom would become a center of communication, a publishing house, a multimedia art center, and a research center that could call upon the resources of the Library of Congress and the Smithsonian Institution. Yet today computers are ordinary for kindergartners, and it is proverbial that junior high students know more about them than their teachers do.

The electronic world provides profoundly new challenges to education that both confound all of the other problems and provide hope for solving them. Schools must incorporate computing into everyday functioning and prepare students to live in an adult world where computing is pervasive. That is not the same as simply buying computers for students. Yet many schools have been incorporating computers as they would new textbooks or laboratory equipment, or adding new classes to curriculum or new departments with specialists hired to teach new subject areas. The institutional structure of schooling remains unchanged, from the way space and time are organized to the evaluation of performance; from methods of instruction to how students are expected to communicate with each other, their teachers, and people outside the school community. Computers become an add-on. In computer labs, machines are lined up in a spare room and used for drill and practice in arithmetic and language arts, or as rewards for students who do their other work quickly and well. Computer "keyboarding" classes, nominally part of newly developed computer departments, are actually replacements for typewriting classes and have nothing to do with computing per se. And advanced computing classes are restricted to students who do well in other subjects, as if that kind of school success were a prerequisite for functioning effectively in cyberspace.

In these contexts, it is common to find the graphic, sound, and other interactive capabilities of computing neglected or relegated to art classes or extracurricular activities. Often a testing session in front of a computer becomes a substitute for discussion and personal interaction, thus using the computer to replace, not enhance, the heart and soul of decent education.

It is senseless to place blame for the misuse of computing in schools. Institutional inertia and the untested nature of computing in education make it very difficult to see how schools can be persuaded to restructure themselves without having models to go on or examples of how computers can be used and schools redesigned. Innovative models will emerge and indicate new ways of organizing learning. With these fundamental reorganizations and their effect upon student performance, the quality and sophistication of learning will themselves become positive forces for school restructuring.

This is why the six models presented in this book are so important. They provide examples, in the context of schools in some of the most underserved and neediest of American communities, of the effective and creative integration of computing into the restructuring of schools.

In order to understand the educational potential of the computer as a tool for learning, I have found it useful to think first about other common tools found around the classroom: pencils, paintbrushes, staplers, rulers. When I got my first classroom computer (an Atari 400), I had to figure out where to put it and how to integrate it into my curriculum. My classroom, a combined kindergarten and first grade, was organized into learning centers. Should the computer go into the writing, the math, the science, or the art learning center? I rephrased the question by thinking of other tools. I did not confine pencils, paintbrushes, or rulers to one center. They were useful everywhere. My one stapler moved from center to center; the computer could do the same thing. (It would have been wonderful to have a portable in those days; instead, I put the Atari with the other reference material and students took turns using it for their individual purposes.)

From the beginning, my students understood that computers could use multiple forms of expression—letters, graphic symbols, drawing, painting, video, sounds, numbers—and mix and match them. Their understanding of what an Atari 400 *should* be able to do was far ahead of what our 400 could actually do. I am now struck by the fact that the children's conceptions of the computer were already in the Macintosh world and in cyberspace, while the machines of that day lagged behind.

Actually, the analogy of computer as tool is limited. A computer is more akin to a toolbox containing a multiplicity of tools. But even this is inadequate. What a computer can do— what no hand tool can do—is shape the material it is provided with independently of the user, make suggestions, and in many ways approximate the functioning of a mind itself. This makes the computer a quasi-intelligent tool, one that invites ongoing acquaintance. You can figure out the use of a hammer or screwdriver once and for all; maybe you can vary the expected use in some creative way. But it is futile, even silly, to claim to know all that a computer can do.

Like the mind, there is an openness to new use, new configurations and rules, new means of representation, and always new applications. In addition, computers are adept at crossing boundaries. Photos, words, sounds, and so on are all common objects that can be organized, manipulated, and joined to one another with the same general techniques, but in unlimited combinations. This mobility has provided previously unimagined power to the mind to think globally and develop unanticipated connections or contrasts. It can (and most likely will) lead to new ways of telling stories, developing narratives, recording history, and organizing experience. The computer is unique, both a tool and an extension of the mind.

All of this has exciting educational potential. We can (and will) think across subject areas and develop programs to connect learners in complex combinations and at all levels of expertise. With the computer, for example, people can spend more time together in the arts or discussion while simultaneously having quick, efficient access to content material. It provides complex cultural representation in multiple media, and it has the potential for shaping curriculum to the needs of each student, class, or community. In other words, the computer is a potent vehicle not only for remote communication (as we have already grasped) but also for enhancement of face-to-face learning.

School Restructuring and the Integration of Computers into Learning

The exciting educational potential of computing, as enormous as it is, too often comes face to face with the realities of everyday life in the schools. It is not just in regard to computers that we are frustratingly unable to make simple, sensible differences in how learning occurs in schools. Although the current school-restructuring movement has many political faces, there is a common core of agreement on what is wrong with public education. The critique begins at the top, with centralized and overly bureaucratized school administrations; it then proceeds to the level of individual classroom practice.

A major thrust of school reform is the decentralization of public school administration, to increased community- and school-based control of everything from hiring and firing to curriculum, evaluation, and application of total-quality and continuous-improvement techniques. In Chicago, elimination of the central bureaucracy and development of local school governing boards is the most dramatic example of this trend. Other prominent instances are schools with site-based management in Dade County, Florida, and the New High School movement in the New York City public schools.

Decentralization and the use of computers in school reorganization go hand in hand. Record keeping, evaluation, and communication among semiautonomous schools in a given district are facilitated through computer webs. In fact, the move is to replace hierarchical and centralized control by networks of mutually accountable equals. This trend places greater responsibility on the staff and community of individuals at the same time that it provides space for experimentation within a given school.

What is interesting about this aspect of school reform is that computers are becoming commonly used among all the support staff at a school. One often finds that a school's computer experts are the secretaries and aides rather than the teachers and administrators. The ease with which people can adjust to computing without formal training (especially with the Macintosh) is displayed every day in the offices of schools using computers for administrative purposes.

Reorganization of centralized authority is not enough, by itself, to effect educational change. Serious educational challenges must be addressed on a school-by-school and classroom-by-classroom basis. Obviously, meeting all these challenges is no small order. Far too many things need to be done to restructure the public schools to try to tackle them all at once in any school. The most sensitive approaches to school reform begin with a schoolwide commitment to self-criticism, analysis of strengths and weaknesses in a given learning community, and determination to plunge in somewhere to accomplish positive, immediate, and, hopefully, lasting change. All this must be done with the idea that a single change in the way education is done is not adequate, but each instance opens a path to continued change.

This commitment to improve K–12 education is evident across the country. It is particularly admirable since the public schools are the only institutions left in our society that, however inadequately, serve the children of all the people in our society and are expected to do it with equal regard for all children. However, given the discrepancy in resources available from school to school and district to district, and given the traditions of school independence from state and federal control, restructuring differs among states, counties, and schools. There are few places where one can find all the issues addressed in one school or district, and nowhere have all the problems of schooling been solved. But across the country there are examples of the blossoming of excellent practice and the development of models of decency and excellence in education. Not surprisingly, most of these models have taken advantage of the newness of computers in the schools to build larger programs of restructuring around the arrival of these powerful tools.

The importance of models of good practice should not be underestimated. It is hard to create new programs if you have not observed examples in action. This is what might be called the paradox of large-scale innovation. Without models, people are left anxious and directionless, innovation fades, and things remain unchanged. Yet there cannot be models for true innovation since the endeavors are meant to be unique. Educators are often asked to develop programs out of whole cloth, using secondhand descriptions or sketches developed by universities or consulting firms that have not tested the innovations themselves. For that reason, the results of the work done through Apple Computer's Education Grants program have a special importance and urgency for people committed to defending K–12 education by working to improve the schools.

The Education Grants program has committed itself to supporting laboratories where educational innovation can be incubated. This means encouraging people not to be afraid of making mistakes, letting things perk, and trying a variety of ways. It means having the patience to watch ideas play themselves out in practice, and having the critical sensitivity to sort through what works and what doesn't. It is through outside support of this nature that working models can be created, models tried and honed in practice and hence useful for other educators interested in finding ways to use computers in their attempts to solve major educational problems.

The six programs described in detail in this book are unique because they do not merely use computer application programs. On the contrary, they use computers integrally and creatively to help solve some of the major social, cultural, pedagogical, and economic problems facing educators everywhere. This book, then, is not so much about how to use computers in education as about the unique role computers can play in integrated school-based programs in traditionally underfunded and underserved communities. They can be multipurpose tools, enhancing learning, empowering students, and situating educational innovation at the forefront of progressive educational change.

July 1996   Herbert Kohl
Point Arena, Calif.

Introduction

*T*his book is a collection of six stories that focus on how teachers in elementary and secondary schools around the country have moved their vision of how to create exceptional educational opportunities for their students into reality. In the process, they have revitalized curricula and transformed and expanded the boundaries of the learning experience.

Each chapter focuses on a single school and its people, challenges, vision, and strategies. They are representative of the hundreds of schools and educators that have been supported by the Education Grants program at Apple Computer. Each year since 1979, this program has provided equipment and training to schools through a national competitive process. Through this process, we uncover gems: new and veteran teachers and administrators who share an overriding belief that all children can learn and that computers, creatively applied, can serve as powerful tools of change to help students improve academic performance and take greater control over their learning.

While the roots of this book took shape through our experiences working with technology-using educators, the book is not about technology per se. Most of the educators we hear from will admit that they had limited or no experience with computers when we met them. What they did have was something far more valuable: vision, combined with passion, commitment, and an unyielding drive to succeed despite the odds.

While this book profiles educators who have been supported by Apple Computer, they in turn have inspired hundreds of other educators—in their own schools, in their districts, and in schools around the country—to undertake similar efforts to engage students in new ways.

This book, then, is both a tribute to their work and a way for them to continue to inspire.

The stories you are about to read are told through the voices of the teachers, students, and administrators who shaped, implemented, and took part in the projects that are described. We wish to acknowledge their tremendous efforts, while also revealing some of the obstacles they, and many others like them, face while dealing with substantive school change. When asked why they continue to do what they do, one teacher answered eloquently: "There's nothing like that 'aha!' when a student is in the process of learning and discovering."

This book is intended for anyone interested in reading about education and how educators and other stakeholders have successfully brought about change in a variety of settings under very difficult circumstances. It is also intended to show the diversity of regions, people, and uses of technology that have enriched these stories.

Each chapter in this book focuses on a particular strategy, or theme, that drives the work of the featured school. Together, they reflect many aspects of current thought on what it takes to create meaningful and engaging learning experiences to prepare students for fulfilling lives in the Information Age.

Chapter One describes a project at an all-boys high school in Newark. It focuses on the development of an interdisciplinary curriculum on contemporary urban issues. Teachers there have developed an interdisciplinary course called Newark Studies, which combines English, biology, and history. Students conduct field research on issues of relevance to the community, present insights on community problems ranging from AIDS to toxic waste, and use simulation software to design cities. The emphasis is on writing and critical thinking, making connections between classroom learning and real life. The end-product of this semester-long course is the publication of *Newark InDepth,* a professional-quality desktop-published magazine that is sold and distributed to residents of Newark.

Chapter Two focuses on incorporating multiculturalism into the social studies curriculum at an elementary school in Abita Springs, Louisiana. Students collect and write stories, develop multimedia presentations, and create a CD-ROM encyclopedia for local residents, utilizing the rich folklore of Abita Springs and the surrounding region. The notion of textbooks and teachers as sole deliverers of knowledge and information gives way to active participation by parents and other residents in the education of their children. Now students see themselves as part of the curriculum and know their significance in history.

The story in Chapter Three demonstrates how one teacher, Concetta (Tina) Petrone, revitalized an inner-city science curriculum at her alma mater, South Philadelphia High School. Known as "High School for the Stars" in its heyday, the school was plagued by delinquency, declining student achievement, and low staff morale. Petrone's vision for creating an interest in science began with a project called the "Computer Greenhouse Effect" and grew to something far more than that. Her determination, commitment, and ability to leverage resources helped build community within and outside the school. A classroom greenhouse provides a laboratory for cultivating plants and conducting experiments and analysis, using the computer as a lab partner. Students conduct research using on-line databases, and produce newsletters about their greenhouse and community-service projects. While Petrone is the "architect" for these innovations, she says that the project depends upon the active involvement of an entire community.

Chapter Four is the story of Dos Palos High School, which serves a rural, isolated community in the San Joaquin Valley of California. Unemployment there is 6 percent higher than the state average, farming jobs are quickly disappearing, and the jobs students might pursue in agriculture and related industries demand sophisticated technological and academic skills. Teachers and administrators illustrate how this community is poised for the future by developing a complex web of activities that focus on career and community. A schoolwide effort led to revised curriculum, technology infusion across all subject areas, career planning, school-to-work opportunities, and lifelong learning choices for students. Teachers and administrators tell how teachers, students, business representatives, and residents form a community of learners reaching for a common goal: to improve the economic, social, and general well-being of their community.

In Chapter Five, you read about an unusual school-within-a-school in central Harlem, where elementary school students are actively involved as the "shapers" of their own education. At the Ralph Bunche School, what began as a study of weather, using a local area network, has evolved into a technology-intensive environment where extensive use of telecommunications—including the Internet—has helped shape new roles for teachers and helped students share knowledge and life stories with other students around the world. Among the voices in this chapter are those of graduates of Ralph Bunche who reveal the impact that this kind of innovation has had on them.

Chapter Six takes you to a Native American reservation in Pine Ridge, South Dakota. Students there are expanding their world and sphere of influence via multimedia and telecommunications. The study of Native American myths and legends has led to joint CD-ROM and research projects with educators and students from other parts of the country, enabling students to apply their own expertise in curriculum development. In this environment, the students' strengths are emphasized regardless of past histories of academic failure.

Throughout the book you will both read about the work of educators and their students as well as *see* examples of student work. Given the tremendous potential of computer technology to help students express themselves—in a wide variety of media—we felt it essential to showcase their creativity, their insights, their humor, and, ultimately, their self-esteem.

This book is dedicated to the many educators supported by Apple Education Grants, whose vision, passion, and leadership helped inspire the writing of this book.

Acknowledgments

I would like to acknowledge the contributions of those who helped make this book a reality, beginning with the students, teachers, and administrators featured in the book. Without you, and the support of your school districts, this book would not have been possible. Your passion and dedication help fuel my own and give me hope. To Mary Furlong, Shelley Goldman, Ted Jojola, Henry Ingle, Vinetta Jones, Madalaine Pugliese, and Paul Trachtman, thank you for helping me with the Education Grants program and for your support in developing the vision for this book. Thanks to my parents, Andrew and Ruth Gonzales, for instilling in me the values of learning and sharing. Fred Silverman, thank you for your belief in my vision, your time, and your incredible support of and contributions to this project. Joy Modesitt, you were a delight to work with. Thank you for your professionalism and commitment to high-quality design concepts. Jenny Abbe and Cynthia Wilber, your time and contributions greatly enhanced the storytelling; thank you. Thanks to my friends at Apple, who helped with some of the finer details and who provided moral support along the way: Timothy Chan, Marcia Griffin, Diana Henneberry, Maria Rose, and Anne McMullin. Lorraine Aochi, you have my heartfelt appreciation and respect for championing the publication effort. Lou Tomafsky, thank you for being there in the beginning and for introducing me to Lorraine. And thanks to my family and friends, especially my husband, Barney.

The Author and Editor

*A*ndrea Gooden was program manager for the Education Grants program at Apple Computer, Inc.for ten years. She has served on the California Governor's Blue Ribbon Commission for Technology in Education and has a California Lifetime Elementary School Teaching credential. Gooden has worked in the British primary schools and in elementary schools and community colleges in the San Francisco Bay Area. She currently resides in Daly City, California, with her husband, Barney, and stepson, Victor Makai Gooden.

Fred Silverman is senior manager of Apple's Worldwide Community Affairs department. He is a former journalist and public relations professional and resides in San Francisco.

CHAPTER 1

Newark Studies: Writing About Community

St. Benedict's Preparatory School

Newark, New Jersey

We hope our students will become a new urban generation of highly skilled youth with a better chance of a college education and an informed voice in shaping Newark's future.

> Keith Corpus,
> ENGLISH DEPARTMENT
> CHAIRPERSON

T he headlines tell stories of poverty, violence, discrimination, and contamination: "Youth and Weapons: A Deadly Combination," "Why Subsidized Housing Is Subhuman," "Air Pollution Is Conquering Us," "Stop the Stats: The Rising AIDS Crisis." But they do not scream from the pages of a big city daily; they are found in a professional-quality quarterly

Newark InDepth, a product of the Newark Studies project, is a professional-quality magazine written and produced by tenth-grade students at St. Benedict's.

called *Newark InDepth.* It is produced by tenth-grade students at St. Benedict's Preparatory School in Newark, New Jersey.

Complete with glossy cover, a competitive newsstand price, and a circulation of one thousand, *Newark InDepth* is the product of an ambitious curriculum called Newark Studies. Combining the subjects of English, history, and biology, the semester-long course focuses exclusively on topics relevant to the city.

"Our thinking early on was that Newark Studies was supposed to be empowering," explained English teacher Keith Corpus, one of three young faculty members who created the innovative course. The teachers believed students could improve their writing and critical thinking skills and become a powerful voice for change if the teachers engaged their students in a cultural, historical, and scientific exploration of Newark.

"We saw the possibilities: students interviewing community activists, politicians, and their neighbors about local issues," said former history teacher Jack Dougherty.

What Newark Studies and the student publication have succeeded in doing is to put a spotlight on a community struggling to revive itself, bolstered by the hope and determination of its youth.

St. Benedict's comprises sturdy brick buildings and a cathedral perched on a slight western rise above downtown Newark. It was first established in 1868 by German Benedictine monks to serve a growing immigrant population. At that time, Newark's reputation as an industrial center was well assured; the city ranked third in the nation in manufacturing output.

Nearly a century later, the city had one of the highest crime rates in the country; the heaviest per capita tax burden; the worst housing; the highest rates of venereal disease, maternal mortality, and new cases of tuberculosis; and was ranked seventh in the number of drug addicts.

Entering the 1990s, the city reflected equally startling statistics: the country's highest incidence of car theft, the fifth highest number of AIDS cases, and the highest level of dioxin ever detected.

Against this backdrop, St. Benedict's has endured as a spiritual and intellectual refuge. It was once known as *the* elite white Catholic school in northern New Jersey. Now its five hundred students, all male, are mostly drawn from the black and Hispanic neighborhoods of Newark. It is one of the most competitive schools in the region, both athletically and academically, with 85 to 90 percent of its graduates continuing on to college and a long waiting list of potential students.

In early 1990, Dougherty, Corpus, and biology teacher Jeff Reardon set out to redesign the school's tenth-grade curriculum in a way they believed would help students master their own environment. Inspired in part by the possibility of receiving a technology-and-planning grant from Apple, the teachers developed a curriculum based on three principles: a commitment to interdisciplinary teaching, a focus on local urban issues, and a strong emphasis on writing and critical thinking skills.

"We were very committed to breaking down what is called the 'shopping mall high school,'" Dougherty explained. In that model, students move "from store to store, not doing any concentrated, rigorous, integrated thinking. We wanted stu-

Convocation

Every school day at St. Benedict's Prep begins with Convocation, a collective event that serves to underline the school's sense of brotherhood and purpose. The young men of St. Benedict's crowd the bleachers in the old gymnasium and spill onto the polished floor as jazzy hymns are played on an upright piano.

As the music ends, attendance is counted off by a representative from each class, and the students begin their impromptu announcements. "Please pray for my sister. She just had a six-pound baby girl," a student declares, followed by supportive applause. Another asks to have his jacket returned from whoever "borrowed" it. (The St. Benedict's community is built on trust, and "lockers" there remain *unlocked*.)

Another youth rises to tell a horrifying story in short bursts. The previous weekend a friend of his was carjacked. He tried to resist and as a result "had his brains blown out." The student body takes it in, registering a universal, if not unfamiliar, regret with silence and nodding.

After more announcements, Father Ed takes the floor. With his wiry vitality and sometimes stern demeanor, he sets the moral tone and the energy level—which is extraordinarily high. In the words of one staff member, he is "a forceful figure," and with little effort gets the full attention of his audience. On this morning he issues a serious warning about an upcoming "dress down" day: students "may not wear more than one earring." The audience titters as Father Ed quickly booms, "This is NOT Halloween." He pauses and glares sternly at his now hushed audience before signaling the end of his remarks—and Convocation—with a sweep of his cassock out the door.

dents to make connections from subject to subject and to apply what they were learning in the classroom to their daily lives."

"Our vision focused on writing across the curriculum, utilizing Apple technology as a tool," Corpus said. "We hope that

by learning to write well and to write persuasively, our students will become a new urban generation of highly skilled youth with a better chance of a college education and an informed voice in shaping Newark's future."

Father Ed Leahy, the school's headmaster, was characteristically supportive of the plan. According to Dougherty, "Father Ed held the leash and let us run as far as we wanted." As it circulated among the faculty, the Newark Studies proposal generated so much enthusiasm that the team decided to implement the new curriculum regardless of the outcome of the Apple grant.

Excerpts from "Communication You Can Swing To"

Students Corey Harris and Nixon Kannah collaborated on an extensive article that represented a departure from news stories typically found in *Newark InDepth*. The young men traced the history of African American music from the time of slavery to the present day and developed a graphic time line depicting the evolution of spirituals, blues, jazz, and rap. Harris and Kannah interviewed preachers and elders from local churches to get their insights on how social and historical events helped give birth to new music forms. Following are excerpts from the article:

Today many people talk about the so-called "old time religion" which originated during slavery. Many slaves expressed their sorrows through the weary cries of pain and bondage. Singing released the slaves' tensions; the songs took their minds off the troubles they were going through. Many slaves on the plantation would sing songs giving the runaways instructions on how to avoid being recaptured. . . .

Gospel Music is more of an international music invented by blacks but it is shared by many people. Many people used the Gospel Music as an opportunity to ask God to do something for them. Songs like "Lord Keep Me Day by Day" are nothing less than a perfect example of them asking God to help them with their problems, such as poverty, segregation, discrimination, crime, drugs, etc.

During the early 1900's a new form of music burst on the scene. Jazz greats such as Duke Ellington started "to jazz" with popular lyrics such as "It don't mean a thing if it ain't got that swing."

Then came the new stuff that has all our youth dancing and prancing around. Rap, R&B, pop, soul, reggae, and funk are all descendants of their ancestors: spirituals, jazz, blues, and gospel.

Even though the music today is expressed differently it still portrays the same characteristics as the music of its ancestors and is still used for the same purpose, that purpose being communication. Blues singers succeeded in singing their problems away which is nothing more than what the controversial rap group Public Enemy does in songs like "Fight the Power." This brings us to the question which gave rise to this article: "Is it Black Music or is it Black Communication?"

NEWARK INDEPTH, WINTER 1993

In May 1990, Newark Studies was introduced during the school's annual "spring phase," a four-week period when students focus on a specific project or community service. Corpus, Dougherty, and sixteen St. Benedict's students chose to do an investigation of the 1967 Newark riots, and the teachers began implementing the strategies described in the Apple grant proposal.

The students developed story ideas, interviewed local residents, wrote articles and commentary, designed layout, selected photographs, and developed a marketing and distribution plan. Within a month, they had published the first issue of *Newark InDepth,* subtitled "An Informative Magazine Written by Newark's Youth."

When teachers later posted a number of positive and critical letters from readers on the classroom walls, one student exclaimed, "Oh my God, people really read our stuff!" Suddenly, the students had an audience. "It was so much better than knowing that, as a teacher, typically I'd be the only one who'd ever see their writing," said Dougherty. "We saw kids taking pride in their writing."

In June 1990, Apple agreed to support the program, and Newark Studies became a required course for all tenth-graders. An old science lab was transformed into a "writing center," with over a dozen networked Macintosh computers set up for composing stories, scanning, creating illustrations, and designing pages.

The team's philosophy was that technology must be adapted to fit the curriculum, not the reverse. "It was a conscious decision on our part not to call it the computing center," explained Corpus. "The writing is the focus." Dougherty warned of the risk of getting so involved in the technology that

The Writing Center.

you lose sight of the educational purpose. "Computers are a great motivating tool," he said. "Basically what we were doing was expanding the word processing revolution."

The teachers of Newark Studies share three classrooms on the school's third floor, including the Writing Center. Each conducts separate classes in history, English, and biology, and participates in common units of study ranging from AIDS education, city planning, and toxic waste to the historical impact of area churches. Students attend three consecutive forty-five-minute classes daily, with two classes in session at any given time. Teachers alternate a planning period, often visiting the other classes to take notes and get ideas.

On the first day of class, teachers introduce the students to the Macintosh by presenting their course outlines on Hyper-Card* software. Most tenth-graders at St. Benedict's have limited experience with computer technology. During the first week, after they receive some initial training and pass a technology "road test," they are issued a "Macintosh Operator's License."

In answer to the inevitable student question "Why does the biology teacher need to see my writing?" teachers and students discuss the principles of interdisciplinary education. "It is common to assume that writing is the exclusive domain of the English teacher," Dougherty said. "Writing doesn't belong just in the English department; it belongs across the entire curriculum."

In Newark Studies, instead of one teacher instructing fifty students how to write, there are three teachers. "There's a big difference when you go home for the weekend with a pile of drafts," Dougherty explained. "You can get through sixteen drafts and make substantive comments, and work with a couple of kids who are really struggling here and there."

One of the mainstay teaching units the team has developed is AIDS education. The subject provides a natural link between disciplines and is particularly relevant for Newark, which has one of the fastest growing populations of HIV-infected people.

---

*See the Glossary of Terms at the end of the book for an explanation of selected terms.

Keith Corpus and students.

A *New York Times* article about the HIV subculture may be the starting point for a history class discussion about the lifestyle, education, and economics of drug users. In biology, the students discuss cell formation and the immune system, referring back to lifestyle issues raised in history. In English, the students are assigned to read an editorial by author Randy Shilts in *Sports Illustrated,* and to answer the question "Why can Magic Johnson play an important role in the battle against AIDS?" Writing assignments are given in each class. Student essays may range from a discussion of HIV-infected babies to a theory on the origin of the disease.

Tom McCabe's history class uses the Writing Center for a discussion on neighborhoods, the primary focus of a Newark InDepth *issue.*

Throughout the semester, students conduct research and interviews, run computer simulations, practice short writing assignments, and learn the principles of peer editing. Teachers share articles, journals, and excerpts from printed work and suggest resources for investigative inquiry.

The final month is reserved for magazine production. In a student-run editorial meeting, classmates decide on a theme for their issue of *Newark InDepth.* Every student's story must be backed up by at least one interview, and each student is responsible for photos or graphics to illustrate his story.

Dougherty recalled a student who was very reluctant to participate, even in the midst of "the Writing Center frenzy" of magazine production. "We didn't know if he was going to get an interview and an article idea that was coherent, in time or

not. The absolute last day he could, he had an idea. He finally got off the phone, slammed it down and said, 'Got an interview, Mr. D.' Here's a kid all of a sudden connecting with people."

The students often work in pairs and teams, and the responsibility for coming up with story ideas and for writing is shared. Fifteen-year-old Alex Echevarria talked about the process with his eyes locked on a Macintosh screen, editing an article that he and fellow classmate Miguel Martin wrote about car theft in Newark.

"It's like clockwork," explained Echevarria. "You've got to be on the same pace everybody is on. You can't fall behind like in other classes." When the result is a story published in a professional-quality magazine, he said, "you feel on top." For this article, Echevarria interviewed two car thieves. It begins with a sad commentary on Newark:

> Newark is known all around the country as the car theft capital of the world. Some people feel disgusted that the city they grew up in is only known because of car theft. . . . Car theft has had a big influence on teenagers. . . . It is even more difficult for a teenager to stop stealing cars after your friends admire you. . . . "I'm the best of kings," Robert claimed with a smile of pride on his face.

Students Rahshan Deane and Antoine Amay provided a stark picture of drug selling in Newark in an article featuring interviews with four teenage dealers. Fifteen-year-old Stacey had been selling drugs for a year:

> Stacey's main goal is not all about money, but also to be well known. She wants to have power and respect among the community. She said she wanted "to be like the others and to be big time."

Another dealer, "Shag," told the student reporters that drug selling is "just a game of survival. I like living my life dangerously. Danger is fun to me." They concluded their profile with another searing quote:

> Shag knows that selling drugs is wrong, but it seems to be the money that has kept him continuing. He said, "I will keep selling drugs until I get caught. Ain't nowhere else you can make money like this. All you do is risk getting arrested or killed. You get to go to work when you want."

Father Ed concedes that the school faces an ongoing challenge in countering the influence of Newark's drug culture. Many of his students, he said, come from neighborhoods that have been devastated by drug and alcohol abuse. "It's tough for a teenager to come here and keep his mind on academics when so much of that is going on."

In Newark Studies, students confront these critical urban issues head-on, drawing on the community for much of their course material. "Our students talk to civil rights lawyers who want to improve urban schooling, city officials who try to make sense out of affirmative action, and neighbors who are really angry about the drugs sold in the playground and want it stopped," said Dougherty.

One of the groups with which the teaching team established a partnership is the Ironbound Community Corporation, an organization that takes its name from a Newark neighborhood well known as a site of toxic contamination, and where a number of St. Benedict's students live. The organization has helped Newark Studies students in their investigations of local industries suspected of contributing to high levels of dioxin and other dangerous chemicals. As a result of their reports in *Newark InDepth,* the students were featured in a PBS documentary, "In Your Own Back Yard," about neighborhood toxic waste sites in the New York and New Jersey region.

The public's response to the magazine adds an important dimension to student work. At the end of the semester, students participate in "Newark Studies Night," when local newspaper reporters and university scholars are invited to join parents, students, and teachers in a critique of the magazine. "The public is rarely exposed to student academic performance,"

Dougherty said. "Teaching is traditionally a private interaction between teacher and student. The public is invited to sporting events, and the student athlete can see right away if he made the goal or not. In Newark Studies, a student's work is seen by teachers, peers, and people outside the school."

"The best thing is, we get to write a magazine," said Eze Nwachukwu, a sixteen-year-old native of Nigeria, with a smile of self-satisfaction. "We get the chance to experience what it feels like to be a reporter."

Coordinating the teaching of urban issues across three disciplines and constantly incorporating new material are ongoing challenges for the Newark Studies team. Students are often

Multicultural Curriculum

While the issue of multiculturalism was being hotly debated in the Newark public school system, student André da Silva discovered that multicultural education had been recognized decades earlier as a way to reduce the city's ethnic divisiveness but was not pursued.

One of the most surprising things I found while doing research was that the belief that a better education can be achieved through a multicultural curriculum is not new. The "Blue Ribbon Commission" believed in this when they wrote *Report for Action* in 1968. Even more surprising was when Dr. Miller said that some things that the commission found had already been stated, in other reports, over 20 years prior to their investigation. That means that these issues have been known to some people for well over 40 years! And yet they still exist! Homeless people on the streets, high unemployment, low health standards, low educational standards, bad housing, etc. We will not solve these problems until we correct our educational system.

reluctant to investigate the same controversies already featured in previous editions of *Newark InDepth.* According to Corpus, each class wants their issue of the magazine to be "different and special." Faculty advisers have also felt awkward about perpetuating an image of Newark as "this horribly impoverished, crime-ridden place," as Dougherty put it, by focusing on the negative aspects of life in Newark in their publication.

Consequently, the teachers are sent scrambling for new themes and resource material. "Interdisciplinary teaching is tough," said Dougherty. "When you teach traditional English classes year after year, you can teach Shakespeare using the same books over and over again." In Newark Studies, the teacher has to come up with the materials. "You don't order twenty copies of 'Everything You Wanted to Read About Health Care in Newark' from the publisher."

Keith Corpus, Tom McCabe, and Harold Guadalupe (left to right) plan the next day's lesson and decide how to organize student teams for the upcoming issue of the magazine.

Teachers on the Newark Studies team also must coordinate their efforts. "If you want to be good at your teaching, you've got to talk about it with other teachers, and there needs to be time made for that," said Dougherty. The teachers collaborate on course outlines prior to the start of the semester, but finding common times to meet day-to-day is not easy. "Sometimes we have meals together or meet on our own time after school hours," said Corpus, who serves as chairman of St. Benedict's English department as well as track coach. "I had a mini-

Harold Guadalupe reviews drafts of articles written for an issue of Newark InDepth.

break between track seasons," he recalled wistfully, "and that offered me a couple of afternoons to spend more time meeting with teachers and talking. But track season is kicking right back in."

The Newark Studies program faced a big challenge in 1992 when both Dougherty and Reardon left the school to pursue advanced degrees. As the new coordinator for Newark Studies, Corpus had the task of finding two new team members. "When people are thinking about becoming a teacher, this kind of interdisciplinary course is not necessarily what they're thinking about doing," said Corpus. "You have to recruit the right individuals to teach it, and that's tough with something as nontraditional as Newark Studies." He was fortunate to find two teachers from within the ranks of the school's staff who were willing to try the new approach.

Harold Guadalupe, an eighth-grade teacher, had been working on a program to improve the writing skills of younger students using computers. History teacher Tom McCabe came to the position well versed in Newark studies, having written his graduate thesis at Princeton on the social history of the African American family, with a particular focus on the 1967 Newark riots. He previously taught eleventh- and twelfth-grade urban studies at St. Benedict's.

Guadalupe, who teaches biology, acknowledged that it is hard to find a scientific link for every topic in Newark Studies. But like the other teachers, he is enthusiastic. "I like the interdisciplinary approach because it exposes me to different teaching styles. I've learned some from Tom, and I've learned some from Keith."

Guadalupe is a graduate of St. Benedict's and of Swarthmore College. "We put the kids through an experience that we put ourselves through. We think of something we want to do, and we kind of roll with the punches if something new comes up. . . . When I first started it was a little bit scary to think about just shooting from the hip, but it's kind of commonplace now."

McCabe noted that the coordinated teaching approach can often have unintended and positive consequences. "Sometimes you very deliberately go a certain way to make a connection, and sometimes it just happens. That's the beauty of it."

St. Benedict's Revival

Following Newark's 1967 race riots, St. Benedict's became a house divided. By 1972, half of its monks and lay teachers had abandoned the landmark school for suburban New Jersey, and the school was forced to close. A small group of monks and teachers remained, pledging to continue to serve and educate the people of Newark, despite the absence of two key elements: money and students.

Among those leading the effort to rebuild the school was Father Edwin Leahy, an idealistic young seminarian. In less than two years, through the generosity of past alumni and with the combined expertise and dedication of the remaining staff, the school reopened.

After his first semester teaching history in Newark Studies, McCabe devised a unit on the social and cultural impact of churches in Newark. "It made a lot of sense to do it, especially at a school with a spiritual, religious background," said Corpus. "The kids had a lot to draw on from their personal experience."

Students conducted neighborhood surveys, compiled histories of local African American churches, and analyzed the importance of music in the church. "It gave students a chance to explore contemporary issues within a larger context," McCabe said. "The history behind the event. The big picture."

Father Edwin Leahy, who knows each of St. Benedict's five hundred students by name, often visits the Writing Center to chat with students.

It also led them to other lines of questioning: "What were the catalytic events that led to the Newark riots? What were the events that led to the L.A. riots of 1992? The public sees the videotaped beating of Rodney King, and we hear the verdict, but what about the forces that led to the boiling point? What about employment? Housing? Civil rights?"

McCabe suggested that another unit, on housing, would allow students to make connections and hypotheses about current and future housing and population trends by studying demographics, immigration patterns, and population.

Father Leahy acknowledges the extra effort that Newark Studies demands of its teachers, and he is enthusiastic about the results. "I think it's a great concept, frankly. I think it's important for the kids to see the interchange that goes on between adults and be a part of it. Working together in a collaborative effort helps that."

Leahy also believes the urban issues raised in Newark Studies are having an impact. "It's always hard to measure how those issues affect teenage kids," he said. "Sometimes you can't measure it until ten or fifteen years later. But their awareness seems to me to have been heightened, there's no doubt about that."

Guadalupe believes that focusing on issues of immediate relevance to their lives will help students resist stereotypes and consider more options for the future. "There are a lot of negative messages that get sent to them, like: 'Because you're a minority this is the job that you're going to have; because you're a minority a certain percentage of you are going to end up in jail.'"

Some students who had struggled academically in the past "really took off with Newark Studies," Corpus said. One student who came to the course with poor academic skills quickly became a key contributor to the magazine and a resident "computer guru."

"They get kids who hate writing, and through the use of computers, and something concrete at the end, they are writing," said Michelle Lewis, a twelfth-grade English teacher at St. Benedict's, to which colleague Jocelyn Johnson added, "and, they are writing *well*."

History teacher Douglas Sterner noted the impact Newark Studies has had among upper-division students. "We've seen an improvement in the kids we're getting now. They're able to write better than those before."

Many of the staff and students of Newark Studies have extended their use of the technology beyond writing and magazine production. During one summer term, students produced an oral history exhibit for the Newark Library. The multimedia presentation featured images, text, and recorded narration on such topics as the Newark Eagles, an early team of the Negro League, and the local jazz scene of the 1930s and 1940s.

Students in the Writing Center also use the technology to produce everything from poems illustrated with scanned-in pictures of girlfriends to business cards and church flyers. Stu-

dents have also used their computer skills to get part-time and summer jobs in the community.

Newark Studies is having an effect on students at other grade levels as well. "Ninth graders know there's this thing called Newark Studies and look forward to their chance to become published authors," Corpus said. Eighth-grade students are learning computer skills as part of a "feeder program," and past students often return to the program to tutor schoolmates on the use of publishing and graphics software.

A collaboration with a nearby middle school gives students an opportunity to pass on what they've learned. In exchange, the Newark Studies team hopes to gain creative technical support from their new partner to expand their multimedia capabilities.

The program continues to provide a variety of opportunities for community involvement. Students who worked with the city's public health department for a series on AIDS education were certified by the AIDS service center as peer counselors. A focus on multicultural education in one issue of *Newark InDepth* resulted in public forums between local officials and St. Benedict's students.

Despite the success of Newark Studies and staff endorsements of the program, Father Ed is not sure other teachers at the high school are ready for the level of involvement Newark Studies demands. "The faculty is the key," he said.

Dougherty noted that Newark Studies team members "used computers in their own education, and it's their natural inclination to use them in teaching." He believes that rather than mandating teacher teams, however, "administrators should encourage opportunities for teachers to choose to work together on designing creative curricula."

Corpus suggests a next step for Newark Studies is to develop an electronic publication to be shared with schools around the world. The future success of Newark Studies, like many innovative programs, is dependent on a number of factors that must continue to work in its favor. It has already survived staff turnover, the ongoing demands of managing new technology, and an ever-changing course of study. Corpus hinted at threats, including the loss of other team members and higher enrollments in the sophomore class, which could necessitate a change in format. But St. Benedict's has a long history of overcoming challenges. "That's the kind of school it is. If you're really willing to make it happen, it will happen," said Corpus.

CHAPTER 2

Hypertext Folklife Project: Culture Becomes Curriculum

Abita Springs Elementary School

Abita Springs, Louisiana

We believe that true learning relies not only on the development of rational, logical, and verbal skills, but on intuitive, emotional, creative, social, and physical skills as well. We recognize the interdependence of the family and community, and the learners' lifelong relationships with the natural and social environment.

The Abita Springs Elementary School Philosophy

29

*T*hey call them "the Florida parishes" because this piney terrain north of New Orleans, spreading east to the Mississippi state line, was at one time part of the vast Florida territory. Lumber companies still regularly harvest and reseed this area, where mineral-laden soil and humid gulf air can make an evergreen seedling explode into a tree in no time.

Here in St. Tammany Parish, situated in a stand of longleaf pines, is Abita Springs Elementary School, a comfortable, clean, and modern set of structures connected by breezeways. In the main office behind the school secretary's desk hangs a slab of polished marble engraved with the Declaration of Independence. On the opposing wall above the copy machine, in fine needlepoint stitchery, is something of a declaration of *interdependence,* "The Abita Springs Elementary School Philosophy," quoted at the start of this chapter. The statement was hammered out by a group of parents, teachers, and staff at the school who were motivated by the belief that education should be directly related to students' lives and their communities. The philosophy emerged as a result of a schoolwide curriculum that draws on local history and folktales to inspire learning, and that uses the computer as the primary tool for organizing and presenting the material.

"What we've done here is build a curriculum around our culture, then enter that culture into computers," explained Kathleen Duplantier, a resource teacher and professional storyteller who is at the center of this revolution in learning. The school's 485 students, about 83 percent white and 17 percent black, provide a potent source of folk history and information on diverse cultures, including French, German, Italian, Native American, African, and Creole.

Abita Springs Elementary School.

According to Duplantier, an offhand remark by principal Carol Rogers in the spring of 1989 first put the project in motion. At that time, the state of Louisiana was suffering from the highest unemployment, illiteracy, and dropout rates in the nation. Nearly half the students at Abita Springs Elementary were classified as economically deprived. Rogers, aware of the importance of preparing students for a technological future, told Duplantier, "We've got to get some computers in here."

The school then had only two computers for its twenty classrooms, and the prospect of reaching Rogers's goal of one computer for every classroom seemed distant. "We've always gone to the parents to work together to generate extra money,"

explained Rogers, but the school was already scrambling for resources to equip a new wing of classrooms.

That same day, an unsolicited copy of Apple's Education Grants guidelines came across Duplantier's desk. Motivated by Rogers's plea, she seized the idea and, with the grant deadline fast approaching, began formulating the "Hypertext Folklife Project." The night of the deadline, she tracked down school superintendent Terry Bankston in his front yard to sign the fifteen-page proposal.

The project called for students to collect and write stories based on local folklife, and then transfer them into Hyper-

Kathleen Duplantier

Before Kathleen Duplantier initiated the innovative curriculum based on folklife stories, she was taking it to the streets. "For about four or five years we had a puppet theater in the Quarter," she relates in her smooth Louisiana lilt. "We did a lot of movement, like the Japanese-style puppet show with big masks and gowns. That's how I started getting interested in folktales."

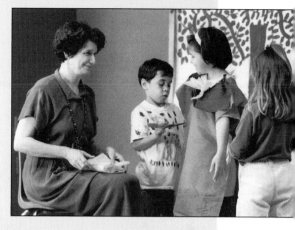

Herself the daughter of two schoolteachers, Duplantier lived in New Orleans with her husband and three children. After one too many burglaries in their French Quarter photography studio, the family moved across Lake Pontchartrain to rural Abita Springs, and Duplantier entered the family business of teaching. In the transition, she lost none of her flair for the dramatic.

"A lot of what I do around here is related to drama," she said, describing her possum costume for an upcoming education conference in Oregon. The presentation included a demonstration of student HyperCard stacks depicting local folktales; it ended with Duplantier, in costume, offering up traditional Mardi Gras King Cake from the podium.

As a McAuliffe Educator, and with her reputation for winning grants, Duplantier is often in demand as a speaker. She has, however, encouraged other teachers at Abita Springs Elementary to share their technology experiences at education forums. "We have had probably ten teachers do presentations at conferences, and every one of them was fabulous," she said. "There are other teachers at Abita that could easily be Christa Educators."

Card "stacks" to become part of a permanent, electronic folklife encyclopedia for the town's school libraries. Duplantier saw it as a way to "sidestep the failure-making school culture," where standard teaching materials don't always reflect reality, and to give students a chance to explore and document aspects of their own cultures. "The shift from the normal curriculum to a folklife curriculum recognizes the students as the carriers of their culture," she wrote.

When the grant came through at the end of the school year, Duplantier was euphoric, but by the time the computer equipment arrived in August panic had set in. "I sat in the middle of the floor and just cried," she said. "I thought, 'I better learn these things fast, because I told them I was going to do all this.' I didn't know anything about all the computers; I didn't even know how to turn them on. It was too much. A few teachers cried with me."

School custodian Cheryl Coakley, whose daughter also attended the school, was instrumental in helping set up and manage the new systems. "She'd sit there with the software and in no time have it all figured out," Duplantier recalled. "She'd say, 'OK, now this is the way you do it.'" By October the computers and the folklife project were up and running and Duplantier was well on her way to mastering the technology.

The school welcomed a steady stream of local residents, visiting artists, and historians who were eager to share their knowledge and experiences. "The greatest benefit is the powerful effect the presenters from the community have had on the students and faculty," Duplantier wrote in an early report on the project. A frequent question became, "Who's coming to our school this week?" As the community and the local press took notice, the favorite question became, "What page of the paper are we featured on today?"

Initially designed to provide an incentive for low-achieving students, the folklife program soon involved children at all achievement levels. Students served as producers and tech-

Hokolonoye'she becomes wolf.

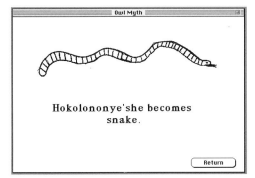

Hokolononye'she becomes snake.

Hokolonoye'she becomes rabbit.

These screens, part of a HyperCard stack created by a fourth-grade class, retell the story "The Hunter and the Owl."

nology assistants, capturing visitors' stories with tape recorders and video cameras.

Duplantier chose HyperCard as the primary software tool for showcasing student work because with it students could combine text, graphics, animation, and sound, creating interactive documents with multiple layers of information. The software's features were adaptable to a range of student skills and learning styles.

One of the last remaining villages of Louisiana's Choctaw Indians was located in Abita Springs, and the culture and customs of the tribe were an early lesson in the new folklife

Jennifer: When and where were you born?

A. B.: I was born in Abita Springs on July 21, 1916, in a little cottage that's still standing today.

FROM JENNIFER KUSTENMACHER'S INTERVIEW WITH HER GRANDFATHER, A. B. KUSTENMACHER

Reginald: Tell me about the house you grew up in.

J. D.: Oh, that house! It was a house! It was a wonderful house. I think about the good old days. Back in those days in time, the house was damp. Oh, but it was built out of good lumber because those houses stood. You can see the moon back out at the sides and watch the hogs and cow walk by. They had shutters like windows—outside shutters. We had to reach out and pull them in. They didn't have the glass windows like we have today, but we enjoyed it. That was back in the '30s. We had to go down to a spring and get water and we had a good time.

FROM "REGINALD TALKS TO PAPA, J. D. THIGPEN" BY REGINALD HICKS

Abita Springs teachers have found another way for students to learn about local history that really hits home: studying the homes of Abita.

During the nineteenth century, Abita Springs was a haven for people fleeing New Orleans from epidemics of yellow fever. Known as the "Ozone Belt" for its fresh air and pine forests, the area soon had hotels and cottages built up around the artesian springs, which were thought to offer a cure for the disease.

The simple "shotgun" and "North Shore" homes were equipped with long side porches to provide sun and fresh air for the sick. It was a distinctive style that later spread throughout the South, and students of architecture still come to Abita Springs to study the originals. As Kathleen Duplantier noted, "Folk built the house. It wasn't an architect who came in and built the house."

Vicki Chauvin's third-grade students, however, are learning much more about the early homes of Abita than just their style. "This is a picture of one of

curriculum. As part of the unit, Choctaw descendants were invited to the school to demonstrate traditional cooking and basketmaking, and a local craftsman offered to help the students build an authentic Choctaw hut.

three houses that a guy built for his three daughters," said student Travis Larkin, pointing to a scanned image on the computer screen. Clicking to the next image, he added, "That's the oldest house in Abita."

The students took walking tours through the town, snapping instant photos of each house and picking out homes to write about. After their survey, they compiled an electronic guidebook to the town on HyperCard, complete with maps, neighborhood tours, floor plans, and historical facts.

The study, Chauvin said, "leads to why the houses were built the way they were and shows what happens to a population over time."

A student in Carol Grow's third-grade class wrote about the railroad's impact on residents, in a book and HyperCard stack the class created and called "All About Abita." During the golden era of the resort town, the train was a primary mode of transportation from New Orleans to Abita Springs:

Everybody used to go down and meet the train. That was the big thrill of the day . . . to go down to see who was on the train, or just watching the train come. There was a depot right in front of Rauch's Grocery Store. That is where everybody gathered in the evening to watch the train come in.

BRIANA ULLOA, THIRD-GRADER

The construction was carefully documented by the students, and their photographs and commentary became the basis for a HyperCard tutorial detailing each step of building

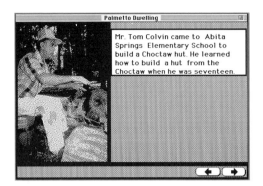

The "Palmetto Dwelling" HyperCard stack integrates photographs and text to guide the viewer through the construction process.

the mud-and-palmetto-frond dwelling. The document is now part of a valuable series of narratives that preserve crafts and customs once common to the area.

Duplantier began keeping a daily journal to chart the development of the folklife project. Here is one excerpt:

On a Friday morning over coffee in the lounge, I heard that at 9:00 A.M. the following was going to happen:

1. King Cake chef is cooking in first grade.
2. A local scuba diver (dressed in gear) is talking to a third-grade class.
3. The fourth grade is making handmade butter to go on biscuits that they will eat with the homemade cane syrup that a father

is bringing. The syrup-maker will talk to the class about making cane syrup.

"Up to this point in the program," she wrote, "I had been planning all the folklife activities. On this day, I was delighted that the teachers were planning on their own."

Teachers began to explore the music and folktales of the local black culture, which have since become part of the school's multicultural curriculum. "We learn folktales that have been collected probably straight off the plantations," said Duplantier. Examples are the stories of "Compair Lapin," the mischievous hare whose "mouth was so honeyed that no one could refuse him anything," according to one of the tales written and illustrated on the Macintosh by a third-grade class.

"Getting the Apple grant gave us the clout to take a giant step toward incorporating multiculturalism into the curriculum," Duplantier said. "There had never been a Black Studies program. The students knew nothing, or very little, about the contributions blacks have made to our community."

A fourth-grader wrote about her conversation with Mrs. Greenwood, a retired teacher who visited the school during "Afro-American Month":

Schools in those days were different than now. She had to walk to school, because they didn't have buses.

In her community the school went up to ninth grade. They didn't have kindergarten. They didn't have lead pencils.

In the town they had movies, but in the country where she lived, they didn't.

Blacks and whites went to different schools. They played basketball, jump rope, and jacks.

She made her living by picking cotton. People had jobs, but not like we do.

In the summer she would can some food and in the winter she would eat the food she canned.

During the summer she would go down to the creek to swim. Their beds were made of straw.

Where she lived there were no machines. They had to make their clothes by hand.

For Christmas some got dolls, some got one cent and they were proud. They had some good times in those days.

April Young, fourth grade

Some of the stories are drawn from books and visiting storytellers, but students also collect oral histories from family members. Student Reginald Hicks interviewed his grandfather, a member of a gospel choir. Duplantier was inspired to make a video about the family as part of a class project.

"He [Reginald] always used to make a tapping noise in class. We didn't know why until we saw this," said Duplantier, referring to footage of the child sitting behind a set of drums, accompanying the choir at Mt. Zion Baptist Church.

Among the stories that are now part of the district's folklife archives are stark reminders of the specter of slavery that marked this region in the past. The following story was told to student Allison Bostick by her grandfather about her great-great grandmother:

My Grandmother's Slave Life

It all started when my grandmother was about 10 years old. My grandfather said that she was slaved in the west. She said the name that her master called her was Thisy. I asked her where did she sleep. She said that she didn't sleep anywhere because she watched the little children. Her father was hung for trying to escape. I asked her did she ever go to the underground railroad. She said that she had never tried to escape. I asked her what did she eat. She said leftovers. I asked her when her master went to church why didn't they try to escape. She said she'd rather live her life being a slave. I asked her did she enjoy being a slave. She said that she had no choice but to be a slave. I asked her did she ever had a good time. She said yes, when I had your great grand-pappy. I asked her where did she have him. She said he was born in a barn. The last thing I wanted to ask her was why did she live so long. But she could not answer.

Allison Bostick, fifth grade

The Hypertext Folklife Project reinforced the school's focus on whole-language learning, a method that puts reading and writing at the center of all learning activities regardless of subject matter.

"Everything is related to whole language," said Duplantier, repeating an assertion often heard from other teachers in the school. When the students in one class wrote about their experiences doing African tie-dye, drumming, and dancing, she explained, they weren't sure what to use as a subject heading on their paper. "What subject was it, anyway? It was art, it was

music, it was social studies, and it was English. It could have been any one of those four."

In another example of whole-language learning, teacher Deidre Sharp's class made "King Cakes," a traditional Mardi Gras pastry, with one student's father, who is a chef. The cooking activity, which students videotaped, also included lessons in social studies, math, and writing. "They experienced it, they touched it, they measured, and they wrote about it," said Sharp. "When they read their own words it's so much more meaningful to them. The folklife curriculum just feeds that."

Duplantier's journal entry about a student in the process of writing up an interview hints at his growing sense of achievement:

> As I type this, Wendell, a third-grader, is sitting next to me with a pair of earphones on his head. He's listening to an interview he recorded with Dick Granier, a crab-net weaver. He is transcribing the tape. This morning he has written four pages. "This is the most I've written in my life," he says to me.

Duplantier strives to maintain a balance between technology and curriculum, seeing the computer as a tool to enhance hands-on learning experiences. "I shiver at the thought of rows of kids sitting all day, being still in front of a computer," said Duplantier. "I would rather see technology as part of a curriculum that understands the whole child."

As an Apple grant recipient and a Christa McAuliffe Educator, Duplantier shares this message with other teachers at educational forums around the country. Armed with lesson plans, student portfolios, and HyperCard stacks, Duplantier challenges educators to integrate the technology in a way that complements their teaching. "I keep saying, 'Where's the curriculum? What are you doing in the classroom? What is this about? Don't tell me you're putting a computer lab in; that doesn't make any sense at all to me. What for? Who's going to use it? What's the whole school about? What's your philosophy?'"

At the beginning of the Apple project at Abita, Duplantier encountered some resistance to the technology among other faculty members. Second-grade teacher Gloria Jones was adamantly opposed to the integration of computers into her lessons. "I was the hardheaded one," she now admits.

After seeing how the technology was being used to improve writing skills and to produce the HyperCard folklife stories, Jones started lobbying for a computer of her own. "I said, 'I don't think that's quite fair. I mean, why do *they* have them?' I whined and complained and she got me one, but it was kind of a dinosaur," she said laughing. "Now I have a little child whose job is to come in every morning and boot it."

Jones's folklife studies center around "Grandmother's Trunk," an old steamer trunk filled with antique kitchen implements, cameras, old photographs, and other items. A teacher or visiting grandparent will describe how each item in the trunk was used, and the students write and illustrate stories about what they've learned and print them out on the computer as little books.

"We asked our visitors at the grandparents' tea how much things cost when they were young," explained second-grader Emily Brown as she flipped through pages of a book the students had made. On one page the teacher had posed related math problems: "How much more do things cost today? Gum today costs 50¢. Gum long ago cost 5¢. Find the difference.

Write a math problem with prices you got from your grandparents."

Duplantier is proud of the way teachers and students have taken the technology beyond just the folklife curriculum. In a project called "Sim-Utopia," teacher Cindy Pharis encouraged students to use the computer as a communications tool. The class sent out electronic messages to seven other schools around the country, setting up a scenario: they were stranded on an island in the Gulf of Mexico, with nothing but a computer and modem and the task of building a utopian culture.

With AT&T footing the bill for telephone charges, students "sent" supplies and suggestions for what they thought would sustain the new utopia. The students then collaborated on a declaration outlining their guidelines for a peaceful society. "It's not a technology lesson; it's a curriculum unit," said Duplantier. "It's the best example of what a teacher can do to take off with the technology."

Angelé McClure, the school's special education teacher, has also seen a change in achievement levels since the introduction of the new technology. "Their love of writing has just been unbelievable," she said of her students, some of whom suffer from severe visual perception problems. "We used to do creative writing once a week, and now they want to do it every day."

As a result of using KidWorks, a computer program that displays symbolic representations of words, McClure said comprehension skills have "just gone through the roof." She described the process of helping one of her students write a story: "We started off with a two-line story. Last week we added a three-line story, and this week we're working on a paragraph," she said triumphantly. "The kids are so open; they're like sponges."

Duplantier has observed the same phenomenon in many classrooms: "The computer has been a motivator. The children are certainly writing more and are proud to exhibit what they have written. Students often reproduce their computer stories as little books they can share with their families. For some, these self-published products are the first books they've ever owned."

"We are all concerned for the children and whatever it takes to get them to learn," said Gloria Jones, who has been at the school since it opened in 1980. "In the past, I've had kids come in here that could not read a word. I don't have those

anymore," she said. "I don't know what's happening, but in this class, all my children are successful."

"For a lot of these kids," said fourth-grade teacher Carol Grow, "it isn't that they're academically weak; it's more about self-esteem. Just not having the opportunity to shine." The Hypertext Folklife Project, she said, "puts them in the limelight."

The folklife activities at the school have also inspired more parent participation. Jonathan Davis is the president of Abita's Parent Teacher Organization. A boat captain who spends seven days on the job followed by seven days at his home in Abita Springs, he is representative of a new wave of parent volunteers at the school. His enthusiasm and energy have helped to involve as many as half of the school's parents in PTO activities.

"I go to each car and look them in the eye and ask them please to come to the PTO meeting," he said, with a crafty smile. "That way they tend to remember it better."

He is proud of the school's achievements and has high praise for Duplantier and her efforts. "Given the background of the kids, I think we do a great job. I read the paper a lot and I know there are a lot of problems, but there are relatively few here."

In addition to raising funds, the parents provide other kinds of assistance, including technical support. As Duplantier noted in a 1993 grant proposal, "a friendly parent-computer-enthusiast is worth more than a busload of highly paid, 'busy' technical supervisors who aren't based at the school."

This was especially true for Cheryl Coakley, the school custodian, who is a parent and a high school dropout; her involvement in the folklife project led to a new career. As an unofficial technical adviser, Duplantier recalled, Coakley "caught on faster than anybody else. Everybody realized how smart she was and somebody said, 'Gee, why aren't you doing something else?'" Coakley took a high school equivalency test and now works full-time as a teacher's aide at another school.

Parents also became actively involved in writing the school's philosophy. It was a "powerful experience," according to Duplantier. In preparation, the committee of parents and staff members studied current theories on multiple intelligences, the effects of technology on education, and a statement of education principles downloaded from a computer network. As a key resource, the parents consulted Howard Gardner's book *Multiple Intelligences.*

"We are considered a rural area," said Jones, "a little stick-in-the-mud school, stuck out in the middle of nowhere. But as you can see, we'll challenge any school."

Three years after the folklife curriculum was launched, the place is humming, and Kathleen Duplantier is at the center of it all. "We have her going in about 250 directions," said fourth-grade teacher Grow, commenting on Duplantier's roles as impresario, storyteller, folklorist, reading specialist, and technical support person.

"Kathleen brings a lot of the fun and excitement into the school," said Jones, on her way back from an assembly featuring a mime troupe from Texas. Other visitors Duplantier arranged for in that week included a group of teenage Gospel singers, a local Creole storyteller, a tie-dye artist, and an African music enthusiast.

Duplantier's enthusiasm is infectious. "At the end of this year we're going to shear a lamb in front of the first-graders," said Duplantier, warming up to her next big project. "Then when they get to second grade, we're going to take them through the whole process—carding, spinning, and weaving—until we get it to a fabric."

It's an analogy that could be applied to all the folklife activities at Abita Springs Elementary, with the end result woven throughout the community: a strengthened social fabric.

CHAPTER 3

Computer Greenhouse Effect: Bringing Biology to Life

South Philadelphia High School

Philadelphia, Pennsylvania

Dreams have come true. Tired, discouraged teachers are revitalized, students enjoy school, new programs have become realities. Students blossomed along with their plants.

Tina Petrone
SCIENCE DEPARTMENT
CHAIRPERSON

*T*hirty-five years after leaving her old neighborhood, Concetta "Tina" Petrone came back to South Philadelphia with high hopes and a deep-rooted understanding of the territory.

"I was born at Eleventh Street, between Fitzwater and Catherine, which in those days was the wrong side of the tracks," said the petite and energetic educator as she negotiated

Tina Petrone.

her Mercury sedan through narrow city streets lined with row houses. "You didn't know you were poor."

Petrone was one of two daughters born into an Italian-American family in the South Philly of the 1940s. Her father, an engineer and inventor, helped spark an interest in science that led to Petrone's early careers in medicine, research, and teaching at the college level.

She then spent ten years moving up through the ranks of the Philadelphia public school system, writing curricula and developing special programs. In 1988, Petrone returned to her old neighborhood as chair of the South Philadelphia High School Science Department.

"It's so funny to think that I'm back here," she said, reminding herself out loud to drive past a cousin's house to check the street address for her Christmas card list. In a running commentary on local landmarks, she revealed a strong and often emotional connection to the area. "The Italians were very proud of their homes," she said, gesturing toward a block of identical row houses. Their front steps were so worked over with cleanser, she recalled, that suds would form when it rained.

Over the years the neighborhood has maintained its status as an immigrant enclave; strong ethnic diversity is reflected in the demographics of South Philadelphia High School's twenty-four hundred students.

But the return of Petrone to South Philadelphia, who at age twelve had moved with her family to the suburbs, got a less-than-enthusiastic response from disillusioned faculty. The science department had been without a chairperson and the school without a permanent principal for six months. The lack of leadership, combined with high student failure rates, poor attendance, and few resources, had left much of the staff demoralized. By the time Petrone and a new principal arrived on the scene, the institution was in disarray.

"The whole science department was so down, they were so discouraged," she recalled. "They crucified me." It was a transitional time in her life on many fronts. "I had a new house, a new husband, a new job. I had a department that was a mess. When they called me Mrs. Petrone, I didn't even know who the heck they were talking about, because my maiden name was Tina Buttacavoli," she related in her animated style.

The day Petrone discovered that the cleaning staff had waxed her medical books to the floor, her patience wore thin: "I said, 'I don't need this,' and my husband said, 'Well, you have to make a decision. You have a choice. You either turn it around, or you walk away.'"

The feisty Petrone didn't back down and instead let her colleagues know that she was in for the long haul. "I said, 'Listen. I am staying. You don't want to stay? I'm staying! I will work with you. I will not ask you to do anything I don't do.'"

She began by cleaning up classrooms, hauling away debris, and refinishing tabletops with the help of her husband, Fred Petrone, and lab assistant Sam Williams. "All of these rooms were decimated," she recalled. "We took bags of trash out. There were roaches all over the place."

In the science department's far corner, adjacent to a third-floor classroom, she made a discovery that would become a turning point for the department. It was an abandoned "greenhouse" complete with plumbing and floor drains—a forgotten room banked by southeast-facing windows that were barely visible beyond the accumulation of cast-off items.

Gazing past the debris, Petrone envisioned a place where students could learn about plant life firsthand. With her customary zeal, she immediately set about restoring the greenhouse. The task proved complicated when she found blueprints showing that the fixtures contained asbestos. The school did not have the resources for complete renovation, so Petrone appealed to her husband for advice. "He said, 'Start writing grants,' and I said, 'How the heck do you write a grant?'"

With his help, and some assistance from the school district, she soon immersed herself in the process of grant writing. Within a few months, the science staff had written seven grant requests, ranging from a few hundred dollars to support student involvement in science fairs to thousands of dollars' worth of computer equipment.

Toward the end of Petrone's first school year at Southern, five grants were awarded on the same day. The most ambitious was a proposal to Apple Computer titled "The Computer Greenhouse Effect."

The project was designed to promote "hands-on activities in botany using Apple computers as learning tools for urban students with extremely limited opportunities to experience 'green.'" It paired students of varying abilities to cultivate their own plants while using computers to record growth data, conduct plant growth simulations, and write detailed reports on everything from photosynthesis to acid rain.

Soon after the grant was announced, the school secured district funds to complete the renovation of the greenhouse. "Everybody was so high, and all the other departments were so envious," Petrone said, almost apologetically. "The comput-

Lab assistant Sam Williams shows off the renovated greenhouse. Hard work, staff support, and district funding made the renovation possible.

ers arrived the same day all the greenhouse supplies came. We had guards all over and (lab assistant) Ed Kelberg was screaming, 'Oh my God, it's happening! Oh my God, it's happening!' That's how it started, and it just kept rolling and rolling and rolling."

Petrone's considerable powers of persuasion were largely responsible for the outpouring of community support that followed. Recruits to her cause included horticulturists from Frank's Nurseries, a local garden supply business, and residents from a local senior center who helped students plant a "tree

A volunteer from the local senior center helps biology and environment teacher John Shevlin and his students plant a community garden.

farm" in a patch of schoolyard turf that had long since given way to weeds and debris.

"To this day, I'd corral the poor plumber," said Petrone, whose irrepressible determination to gather support seems to guarantee the program's success. "That's the way you've got to do it."

Within a year after the greenhouse was established, the students of South Philadelphia High School won awards for every one of their entries at the Pennsylvania Horticultural Society's Junior Flower Show.

The greenhouse program was originally limited to tenth and eleventh graders, but it began attracting the interest of students at all grade levels. The department expanded the curriculum by including outdoor experiences relating to botanical and environmental issues.

Petrone and lab assistant Williams attended local environmental conferences to seek contacts within the community and identify potential outlets for student interest. They invited representatives from several groups and agencies to the school and formed alliances with the Environmental Protection Agency, the Sierra Club, and the Penn State Urban Gardening Program.

Using the computer to organize and analyze their data, students began monitoring the water quality of a local tributary for the Delaware Riverkeeper Network. Others learned how to make nearby residences energy efficient for seniors and low-income tenants through the Neighborhood Energy Center's "Adopt a Row Home" program. As part of this initiative, students ran computer simulations to calculate the amount of energy that would be saved by insulating.

Teachers soon began integrating computer technology and multimedia tools into other subjects. Chemistry students simulated experiments using specially designed software, and students in Sherri Carr's human anatomy class presented their own HyperCard stacks at a health conference. This class was part of the school's new Health Academy, a special interdisciplinary certificate program established by Petrone and Carr for students interested in careers related to health care—a fast-growing job segment in the Philadelphia area.

Teachers Don Snyder and Solomon Sadres received grants to bolster the school's involvement in science fairs. For the first

time in years, students entered experiments in local competitions and used the "greenhouse computers" to create accompanying graphics and posters.

In an interim report on the greenhouse project, Petrone's gratitude and pride were typically unrestrained. "Nothing has or ever will be the same. Dreams have come true," she said. "Tired, discouraged teachers are revitalized, students enjoy school, new programs have become realities. Students blossomed along with their plants."

As the department's remarkable achievements began to be noticed, the school district allocated $300,000 for a renovation of all the science labs and classrooms.

"It took some time for the community to acknowledge that Southern's science students were learning," Petrone said, but when people began to see students out planting trees in the community, and visiting local hospitals and retirement centers, many were inspired to return the favor. "One elderly volunteer stood outside the school and said, 'I could be home making tomato sauce, but no, my husband has me watching him plant a garden with high school students,'" Petrone recalled. Another volunteer serenaded the students with Italian opera as they did their spring planting in front of the school.

In 1991, Petrone was named Pennsylvania's Christa McAuliffe Fellow by the U.S. Department of Education, catapulting her department to national and even international stature. The fellowship, the first given to a Philadelphia teacher, provided funding for a planned "Eco-Science Institute." Patterned after the school's Health Academy, it is designed to prepare students for careers in environmental science.

The Apple grant, Petrone later wrote, launched her into "a universe of technology, professionalism, encouragement, and support." The McAuliffe Fellowship was another ringing endorsement of her grassroots approach to school revitalization.

"This is the nucleus of everything we do," Petrone explains as she proudly leads a visitor into the Apple Science Resource Room. "It's like a little utopia."

In their crisp white lab coats, she and her lab assistants move around the rows of computers, supervising students at work. Potted plants and terrariums in twenty-ounce plastic soda bottles line the wall against the windows. Beyond another set of windows is the greenhouse. Along the wall separating the greenhouse from the classroom are electronic probes for measuring soil moisture and temperature. On the classroom side, the probes connect to several computers that continuously record the climate changes.

Sophomore Clifton Stewart checks the status of his plants after a recent drop in temperature. Like other students of the greenhouse project, Stewart uses the computers to record plant growth and write reports, as well as test out theories using such simulation software programs as Lunar Greenhouse and Odel Lake.

He also tends his plants daily. "I water them, propagate them, and give them plant food," he explains, looking over the shelves of leafy vegetation. Since his involvement in the greenhouse project, he has also taken over the care of his mother's houseplants, and in the summer he produces his own crops of

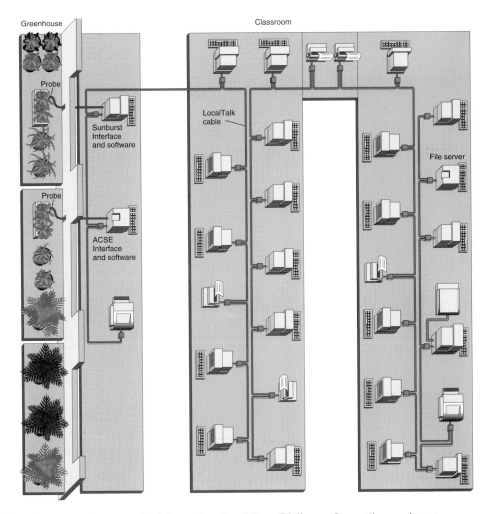

The classroom is networked in a standard LocalTalk configuration using a
Macintosh SE as the file server. The ACSE (Analog Connection for SE) interface and
Sunburst interface are used to take measurements. The computers are capable of
producing, detecting, and storing electrical signals (voltages). Some electronic
devices can produce voltages that are related to such physical qualities as light
intensity, temperature, pH, and pressure. These sensors are connected or interfaced
to a computer that measures and records the voltages produced. These data are
then analyzed and plotted as a graph that can be displayed, printed, or saved to
disk for future reference.

corn, okra, and tomatoes. "My mom doesn't really like plants, so I take care of them," he says.

With the increased focus on environmental issues, one chemistry class was inspired to create a new organization called Students for Environmental Awareness and start publishing a newsletter. "They were studying the Delaware River and the pollution problems in this area. They decided they wanted to spread the word and let other students know about their concerns," said lab assistant Kelberg.

With the aid of a visiting professor, environmental chemistry teacher Howard Branin and his students test a nearby lake for microbes and pollutants.

The first edition of the newsletter featured an open letter to a Pennsylvania senator about water contamination. Another student wrote a letter to then President George Bush about the importance of Earth Day and received a reply. "It changed her life," said Petrone.

When the Health Academy students saw what the chemistry students were doing, they also decided to desktop publish a newsletter. The trend continued, and soon the science department was producing three newsletters.

Students and teachers began using electronic bulletin boards and networks to do research and to establish links with other schools. Through information services such as the Internet, EcoNet, AppleLink, and Learning Link, they shared statistics on water quality and other data. "What we're managing to do is team up with other people," Petrone said. "We're able to take a look at the big picture."

Petrone herself was a computer novice at the beginning of the project—along with most of the staff. "In the beginning of the year, I couldn't get people to use them. I wouldn't touch them either," she admitted. Keeping her vow not to ask others to do what she didn't do, she worked with Kelberg and Williams to set up a network, integrate the computers into the day-to-day classroom routine, and promote computer use among other staff members. By the end of the year, two of her teachers had complained to the principal that Petrone was not giving them *enough* time on the computers.

"The principal called me down, and he was laughing. He said, 'Did you ever think you'd see this?' And I said, 'What?' He said, 'You got reported for not putting them in the computer room.' I thought that was the greatest compliment I ever had. I loved it! I loved it!"

Now she's frustrated by not having more time to spend on new applications. "I need to learn so much more. The kids understand more than we do," she said. "The one thing that many of them cling to is the computer. They can identify with it. They really like it and they're not intimidated by it."

Petrone also manages requests from teachers in other departments who want to take advantage of the technology. In the beginning, she considered limiting the use of the computers to the science department, but Williams and Kelberg urged her not to restrict access. "They didn't want to be isolated, and that speaks well of them," she said.

The science department now actively seeks collaboration with teachers in other departments. Biology teacher Sadres praised the interdisciplinary approach. "This is the integration of biology, science, math, and English, which is really what education should be about."

"We opened it up," Petrone said of the coordinated teaching method. "If the students visit a nursing home with a science class, they keep a log or a diary and the English teacher examines it for clarity. When we introduce ethics, then all of a sudden we're involved in social studies. When we're making dilutions and solutions, then we're doing math."

In December 1992, the Health Academy received another honor for the science department: an official alliance with nearby Hahnemann University Medical School. But other events at the school that day eclipsed this news.

Two teenagers, a girl and a boy armed with a knife and a sawed-off shotgun respectively, confronted another student in the lunchroom, wounding him in the foot. The impact on the school was devastating, as students and teachers tried to counteract the negative images being broadcast about the "shootout."

"All in all, it's a nice school," said fifteen-year-old Jimella Monroe two weeks after the incident, as she sat at one of the computers composing a letter. "It gets a bad reputation from some kids." Framed by a massive avocado plant looming behind her, she wrote to a new pen pal at another Apple Education Grants recipient, Waterford Country School in Connecticut:

> I currently live in South Philly and have all of my life. If you haven't already heard, there was a shooting at South Philadelphia, where I currently go. It was all over the news and in the newspaper. The school gets a bad reputation because of a few students. How is your school?

Although it was only the second incident involving a gun in the school's history (the first was in 1960), the news coverage seemed to confirm a negative perception of the school. Two months after the incident, the principal was granted a sabbatical, effectively ending his five-year tenure, and George Di Pilato was appointed interim principal.

"What occurred was directed at a particular individual over something that happened outside the school," Di Pilato said. "The young man who was shot was involved in some illegal activity outside of school, and someone was determined to get him."

Di Pilato believes that, unlike at some city schools, the threat of violence at South Philadelphia is minimal. "If it were gang violence, then there would have been that aura of fear in the school," he maintained. His view is shared by others, including students, and the occasional sweeps and searches in the months following the shooting yielded few weapons of any kind and no guns.

Lab assistant Sam Williams is a vigorous advocate of the school and its students and is a member of the district attorney's special committee on issues having an impact on youth and seniors. He was instrumental in helping Petrone integrate the computers into the curriculum and believes access to technology is one way to engage students. "One of the things that makes you happy is when you see the final product from a student who was initially rebellious and who had said, 'I'm not going to do that.'"

Williams recalls a visit by a reporter intent on doing a story about conditions in the school's crowded lunchroom. "I said, 'Do you want a good story? Do you want a success story? Let me show you some positive stuff that you can write about that's not hearsay.' She said, 'Well, I'll be back.' She didn't want to hear it."

He knows that some students promote the school's tough image. "They're always going to find something to do to show, 'Yeah, I'm from that school you were talking about.' But you have a lot of good students here who don't see the environment like the outside sees it," he said. "I see different results than what the media come here to see."

The Sierra Club's Richard Meyers, one of the science department's community sponsors, agrees that many people have a distorted view of the school. "Everybody thinks all these kids are running around here like gunslingers or something and they ignore what all these good kids are doing," he said. "That's got to be discouraging to them, let alone [to] the teachers and everybody else."

Meyers has helped organize a number of student activities, including wilderness trips. "Tina is always saying that for a lot of kids their world sort of ends at Broad Street. You go beyond that and you're going off the end of the world, because you don't know what's there," he said. "They are just looking for something to give them meaning in their life. They get in contact with nature, talk about it, write about it, learn about it, and that starts to fill that place in their life."

Don Snyder also sees a reluctance among his students to venture beyond South Philadelphia. "They're so insulated that way. They don't go out of their neighborhoods." When Snyder plans a class trip, students ask him, "Do we have to go above Washington Avenue?"

"I try to put fires under them to make them do things," he said. "Usually I make everyone do some type of out-of-school activity: an energy debate, a science competition, a poster con-

test, a writing contest. That's how you develop relevancy and importance."

Teacher Howard Branin, one of the champions of the Eco-Science Institute, also believes that computers provide a positive outlet. "The kids who work in the computer room see results. The kids who work in the greenhouse see results," he said.

Meanwhile, the department continues to receive grants to bolster other programs. Less than two weeks after the shooting incident, the science department received a $75,000 grant from the State of Pennsylvania for community service activities. A few months later, they were awarded another grant from Apple to help nearby middle schools prepare students for high school by reinforcing science and technology skills.

With the same talent she employs to corral plumbers and community support, Petrone is also reaching outward to other

schools and other teachers. A persistent dilemma is the lack of resources to allocate toward computer training for teachers. "We all have the same problem," she said. "We would all like to learn more, and we're just not getting the time. The only way I can provide downtime or substitute teachers is through grant money."

Petrone and Williams have developed a partial solution to the problem by offering periodic "survival" workshops for teachers, and by developing their own basic computer "help" manual. "We've been fortunate," Petrone says. "I think we've been blessed. This department really works together, and we've had great successes as a result."

Moving down Broad Street past the tall buildings near the city's center, past the historic district where the Declaration of Independence was written, you eventually come to the well-worn landscape of South Philly. At the transit crossroads of Broad and Snyder, a cyclone fence marks the perimeter of South Philadelphia High School.

Originally a boys' school, it was established in 1906 as "Southern Manual Training and High School," and a separate campus was added for girls. The name was later changed to South Philadelphia High School, but it is still referred to today as "Southern."

It is also known as the "School of the Stars." Early graduates included singers Marian Anderson (Class of 1922) and Mario Lanza, followed in later years by entertainers Eddie Fisher, Jack Klugman, Buddy Greco, Joey Bishop, and James Darren.

In 1957, a local television dance show called "Bandstand" went on the air in Philadelphia and was soon broadcast nationally as "American Bandstand." South Philadelphia High School produced some of the most famous teenage heartthrobs of that era, many of whom got their start on the show, including Frankie Avalon, Bobby Rydell, Chubby Checker, and Fabian.

Other notable South Philly alums include National Basketball Association Hall of Famer Eddie Gottlieb; Jerolene Pizzaro Drefs, one of the first women to receive an M.B.A. from Harvard and later vice president and treasurer of *Newsweek*; the president of Greyhound Bus; the head of the New Orleans Opera; and the physician who found the antidote for spinal meningitis. The current South Philadelphia school board president, Andrew Farnese, graduated from Southern in 1933.

A nostalgic undercurrent still runs through the school, a remnant of its glory days kept current by faculty members who themselves attended Southern.

"It was a very interesting place when I went to high school. They were good years," said Principal George Di Pilato, who graduated from Southern in the late 1950s. He is happy to be back at his alma mater. "I'm enjoying it. I've held every position there is to hold in education, so what I do now, I do for love."

Since receiving their first grant, the South Philadelphia High School Science Department has gotten seventeen additional grants and established two dozen institutional affiliations. Colleagues who were once skeptical of Petrone praised her leadership. As if to dismiss her own consummate skills, Petrone offers, "They know I'm totally zany."

The school has steadily lost enrollment in recent years, partly because of competition with several newer area high schools. Many students do not have the benefit of a supportive family structure. "Some of these kids don't have homes or parents," said teacher Branin. "They live as a group, like in Dickens's *Oliver Twist.*"

Other students at the school—including at least three young women in Petrone's class—already have children of their own. "These kids are still children, and they're performing as parents," she said.

"You have to build on your strengths. Tina's program and what she's doing is really the bedrock for Southern's return to prominence," Branin said. "Tina and the entire department have proven that they can grow, and take on more responsibility without getting bogged down. No question about it. It really becomes the hub of the wheel of the school."

Richard Meyers has an appropriate analogy for Petrone's efforts on behalf of students. "I always liken it to seed planting. You plant the seeds and some of them fall on concrete and don't grow, some of them aren't going to be watered or taken care of, but some of them grow and produce other seeds and pretty soon you've got a forest," he said. "A lot of kids are so buried inside themselves that you can't reach them. But there are a lot of kids that are just waiting for somebody to reach out to them."

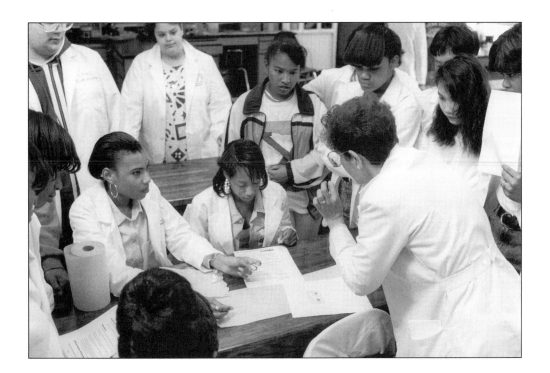

In the midst of the campus furor over the lunchroom shooting incident, one student quietly slipped Tina Petrone a note demonstrating clearly that she is doing just that:

> I would like to say that I am very grateful for you. You are one teacher who cares about your students. Even though a little of this year has only passed and there is still much more to learn, I must say that I love your class. The challenge that you give to your students to dare to be successful has enlightened me more to pursue my goal as a medical technologist. I appreciate what you have done. Thank you.

CHAPTER 4

21st Century Learning: Putting School to Work

Dos Palos High School
Dos Palos, California

A strong back, the willingness to work, and a high school diploma were once all that was needed to make a start in America. They are no longer. A well-developed mind, a passion to learn, and the ability to put knowledge to work are the new keys to the future of our young people, the success of our businesses, and the economic well-being of the nation.

U.S. Department of Labor
SECRETARY'S COMMISSION ON
ACHIEVING NECESSARY SKILLS,
JUNE 1991

77

*A*t first glance, Dos Palos, California, may seem an unlikely setting for high-tech innovation. On approaching the small San Joaquin Valley town of four thousand, travelers are greeted by a yellow highway sign with a silhouette of a farmer on a tractor. Captioned "next 16 miles," the sign warns of a slower pace.

The community began as a ranch settlement in the 1880s, one of several belonging to a local cattle baron whose headquarters were twenty-five miles to the west in the town of Los Baños. Ranch hands dubbed the distant acreage "Dos Palos" for the two trees that guided them to the spot on the otherwise barren landscape.

Now the streets of Dos Palos are lined with trees, and the only things taller than the sycamores and the white spire of a church steeple are three satellite dishes on the roof of the high school—conspicuous symbols of the school's commitment to providing students with broad options in the information age.

"There's not a lot of business here," explained Dos Palos High School Principal Ernie Wall. "This is all agricultural area. Most of our kids who graduate have to leave this area to get a job." During his sixteen years as principal, the unemployment rate in the area has soared, sometimes as high as 26 percent.

Acutely aware of dwindling job prospects for the 650 students of Dos Palos High School—of whom 65 percent are Hispanic, 25 percent Caucasian, and 10 percent African American—Wall and his staff developed a curriculum to prepare students both for college and for an increasingly competitive job market. Their unique combination of rigorous academics and occupational training, supported by the use of new technology, goes a long way toward meeting the challenges set out in the U.S. Labor Department's 1991 report "What Work Requires of Schools."

"All the demographic factors that say you shouldn't be able to succeed doubled, but our college-bound population quadrupled in that same time," said Faye Johnson, director of finance and special projects for the school district. She and Wall worked together to secure grants and other funding to renovate the school, stock the library and other classrooms with books and computers, offer English courses for Spanish-speaking students and their families, and develop a balanced program of vocational and academic training.

"A lot of people ask us how we manage to do all this," Johnson said, as she crisscrossed the campus, careful to avoid construction zones. "If Ernie Wall says it, it gets done. He's just so darn good." She pointed toward the recently remodeled auto shop, a project of Wall's summer youth employment program. "The principal was out here in his hip boots helping with the cement work. That's how we get it done."

Wall is a master of coercive humor, cajoling both students and staff into ever higher levels of achievement. He delights in roaming the classrooms and is somewhat disapproving of administrators who stay in their offices and "play on the computer." It's an attitude that might seem inconsistent with his strong endorsement of technology in education. "He has vision," said Johnson. "I don't know that that man can even turn on a computer, but he saw what the technology could do, years before, and he was determined to provide it for our students." Eventually, she added, people began to catch on to his way of thinking.

"I'm not a big computer user, but I *can* turn one on," Wall said, smiling from behind a desk unencumbered by electronics.

He recently gave his computer to the counseling staff "because they needed it more than I did." This attitude has guided his leadership of the school for the better part of two decades. "This is his little family and he takes care of them," said graphic arts teacher Mae Pierini. "You always know you're going to get the support from him."

Wall cautions other educators not to expect the kinds of changes they have made at Dos Palos to happen spontaneously. "It's a long process that we've done through the years. It just didn't happen overnight."

Soon after Wall became principal of the high school in 1977, the economic realities of the region began to shift radically. Farm income went down, unemployment went up, and more families were living at the poverty level. At the same time, the number of students who entered the school speaking little or no English was growing.

In 1978, California voters approved a ballot measure that forever changed school financing. The passage of Proposition 13, known nationwide as California's "property tax revolt," meant that local property tax assessments would no longer increase with the value of the land, but instead be frozen at 1978 levels.

Before Proposition 13, Wall explained, the Dos Palos High School District could expect an automatic cost of living adjustment of 6 percent every year. "This was a rich farm area," he said. "We could count on that money coming in. Prop. 13 changed the whole ball game. We had to look for other ways to fund our innovative programs."

Since the school's budget would now depend on average daily attendance, Wall made that a priority. "We have a high attendance because we can't afford to lose anybody. We make sure that they're here, or they're in continuation school or independent study," said Wall. "We had to change, and we got in and started making those changes early." The school began to seek grants from a variety of governmental and private sources, learning to consolidate its resources for maximum effectiveness.

One of the strategies was to enroll every eligible student in the Regional Occupation Program (ROP), qualifying the school for extra funding to maintain and expand vocational training and apprenticeships. The school also established itself as a center of learning for the whole community by offering adult education, college extension courses, and English as a second language, leveraging funding for those programs to benefit instruction at all levels.

Changes were also made to boost academic excellence. Graduation requirements were modified to include more math, science, and English. "Tracking" was eliminated, all students were enrolled in college-prep-level classes, and state funds for remedial education went toward a "success lab" for students who needed extra tutoring. "We expect a lot out of our students," said calculus teacher Lana Balatti. "We try to make it a friendly atmosphere, and we make as many allowances as we can to not let them fail—except at their highest level."

Initiatives included a program called the Family English Literacy Project, to help integrate Spanish-speaking students into regular classes more quickly, and to encourage their parents to study English and become more involved with their child's education. Special-education students who had once been bused long distances to county centers were mainstreamed into regular classes.

Teachers also began to coordinate their efforts more. A grant proposal to buy maps for every classroom resulted in increased communication and collaboration, as teachers of every subject from physical education to mathematics began adding geography to their lesson plans. "We said, 'Hey, wow, we can do this interdisciplinary stuff and it works,'" recalled Johnson, who at that time was the school's librarian. "It was a small thing, but it led to much bigger things."

In a project sponsored by the California Academic Partnership Program, the faculty initiated a comprehensive review of all English, language arts, and social studies courses, redesigning them to include career explorations. In conjunction with the state university and a local community college, English teachers at the school developed a curriculum for improving language arts through reading literature. This curriculum is now used by teachers nationwide.

A key component of the school's improvement efforts early on was access to technology. Ginny Farmer, now the school's technology coordinator, returned from a computer trade show in San Francisco in 1984 with two of the first Macintosh computers ever made. Ten years later, they are still in use, alongside newer equipment, in the school's journalism class. "This school has always been amazing," Farmer said, recalling that Dos Palos High School had set a precedent for innovation as early as the 1960s with its own closed-circuit television channel, complete with professional cameras and a sound studio.

Now a room in the school's library is outfitted with video equipment and microphones for receiving live interactive satellite extension courses from two California state colleges. Computers have transformed the school's former drafting shop into a professional design and print shop. In agriculture, wood shop, and welding courses, Macintosh computers are used for everything from inventory control and farm management to computer-aided design (CAD).

In 1990, when Dos Palos submitted a proposal to Apple for additional technology to reinforce links between academics and vocational training, basic computing skills were already included as a graduation requirement. "Few jobs exist today, and even fewer will exist tomorrow, that do not require the daily use of computers and related technology," the proposal stated. "District efforts to date have established the infrastructure of hardware, software, training, and curriculum for basic skills."

Shown left to right: Ernie Wall, Dos Palos High School principal; Ginny Farmer, computer tech support; and Faye Johnson, director of finance and special projects, Dos Palos High School District.

Unlike many schools, Dos Palos is fortunate to have full-time technical support. Ginny Farmer, the mother of two Dos Palos graduates, parlayed her long-time fascination with computers into a position as the school's computer coordinator. Armed with her "tool kit" of diskettes, she reinstalls software, cleans out overcrowded hard drives, analyzes printer errors, and even uses the soldering skills learned in a class on stained glass for repairs.

Farmer first studied computer science in college during the keypunch era. "Back then, one computer would fill a room," she recalled. After moving with her family to Dos Palos, she worked at the local newspaper, where she experienced the transition from the industrial to the electronic age firsthand. "We went from hot lead to a computer typesetter. It was so new that nobody knew how to run it, so I wrote the book, so to speak, on troubleshooting."

She began working at the high school as a teacher's aide and then as a secretary. At about the time Farmer returned to college to continue her studies in computer science, Principal Ernie Wall was strategizing about how to introduce computers into the school. Looking for a staff member to help coordinate the effort, Wall was told, "Well, Ginny's taken a class." As he put it: "History was made."

Now, Farmer not only manages technical support at the school; she also teaches computing basics at the college level, and her reputation as a technical wizard has spread to the community at large. It's not uncommon for Farmer to be summoned to the local hospital to diagnose an electronic glitch.

"I just have a really great time," she said. "They pay me money to play with computers all day."

Titled "Teaching for Transition to the Next Century," the Apple grant proposal promised to give students a "lifetime warranty," certifying their preparation for the world of work and making all teachers, in effect, vocational advisers. After the proposal was accepted, the school began to expand its original objectives. "It takes time to build from one program to the next program and figure out what works," said Johnson. "When we wrote the Apple grant, we weren't yet thinking about 'career paths.' We were just thinking about every student graduating 'job ready.'"

The Career Path program that evolved out of the Apple grant proposal encourages students to begin planning for college and careers before they even enter high school. "They bring the eighth grade over to spend two days in the Career Center and we ask them to choose a Career Path," explains counselor Nihla Maron. "Early on, we try to get a sense of direction." The files are updated throughout high school so that by the time a student graduates, five years of career and college interests have been charted.

Students also earn certificates of mastery in specific skills related to agriculture, art, or industrial arts—the three categories identified as having the best opportunities for employment in a survey of entry-level positions within a seventy-five-mile radius of Dos Palos.

One of the most popular occupational courses at Dos Palos High School is graphic arts. "Basically our students are getting all the fundamental skills they need to enter the graphic communications industry," explained teacher Pierini, who is herself a graduate of Dos Palos High School. "We do desktop publishing, we do our own line films, we burn our own plates, and we print," she said.

As part of the course, students offer graphics and printing services to local nonprofit organizations in a process designed to mirror that of the actual workplace. "If a customer such as the Kiwanis Club comes in and needs tickets for a dinner dance, I may pick Cindy and say, 'This is your customer,'" Pierini explained. "She's responsible for finding out what the customer needs, just as she would be in the real world." If her students were to miss a deadline for a customer, she said, they would

Graphic arts teacher Mae Pierini assists a student with silk-screening, one of many skills taught in her class.

flunk. "In the real world they do flunk. If they don't do it, they get fired." Fortunately she's never had to enforce the rule.

Pierini's students also print the school newspaper. "If it's Dante's turn to be in charge, he gets a crew of three additional students, and he's responsible to see that it's done. At the completion of it he grades his co-workers, just as a supervisor would."

Pierini often promotes her students' skills and services in presentations to local nonprofit organizations. She avoids competition with professional print shops, but occasionally students will extend their services to local for-profit businesses, she said, because "we don't have any printers in town."

Along one wall of the graphic arts room is a row of Macintosh computers and a door leading to a darkroom. Drafting tables are clustered in the center of the classroom, and in the back of the room is an offset printing press. The walls are decorated with silk-screened T-shirts, posters, and many other examples of student design work.

Pierini starts out the course with freehand drawing assignments using pen and paper; then she gives students the same assignment on the computer. "They start playing, and they see how quickly they can do something that looks professional," she said. Many of her students have won awards for their computer design work.

"I look forward to the two hours here," said senior Anna Hernandez, who plans to study advertising and graphic arts in college. Her portfolio includes illustrations and renderings as

Senior Anna Hernandez displays work from her portfolio, including not only a printed piece but also the film and printing plate used to produce it. All of these materials were created in her graphic arts class.

well as award-winning computer graphics. "She [Pierini] lets us work by ourselves and try to figure out things on our own. But if we need her, she's there."

Senior Roman Reyes used his graphics and offset printing skills to create a business card for his sideline as a freelance disc jockey, and Diego Meraz was inspired to pursue a career as an architect. "I like to draw, and it just popped in my head to go after it," he said.

In Darrell Darnell's drafting and wood shop class, students learn the principles of CAD by drawing up house plans, cabinets, and coffee tables on the computer before ever sawing a board. Darnell acknowledged the benefit of learning freehand board drafting; but in the work world, he said, computer skills are more relevant. "There's nothing happening as far as the industry on the board anymore. It's all CAD. Even on the farm now they're not going to be working without a computer."

In agriculture, instructors Howard Lewis and Don Frey use the Macintosh for everything from cataloging tools and commodities trading to designing farm equipment. Students use an on-line service called Agri-Data to get grain reports, check on cattle markets, and access detailed reports on such topics as how flooding in Iowa is affecting corn prices. With a

growing interest in international agriculture, students also chart shifts in global markets and track companies on the New York Stock Exchange.

"Howard revitalized it, got students interested in Ag again," said Johnson. The ability to get such a wide variety of current information off the computer has helped renew interest. "There's a lot of material out there that's very useful," said Lewis. "The kids have access, and all of a sudden they're developing their work off of that. You're expanding the kids' horizons from the San Joaquin Valley, to California, to the United

States, to the world. They're asking, 'How is NAFTA going to be affecting California?'"

As in wood shop, student welders use the computers to sketch out their designs for flatbed trailers and weight benches before assembling them. With an assortment of high-tech welding tools as well as computer technology, the machine shop has a workplace atmosphere. "If they walk into a shop outside of here, it's the same environment," said Frey.

The teachers work together to link vocational skills to academic subjects. "There's been talk back and forth, since this grant, about vocational versus academic," said Ginny Farmer, "but students use both their academic and their vocational classes to help them gain their goals."

Dos Palos math teacher Paul Chounet developed a practical algebra course that applies abstract mathematical principles to welding, agriculture, and other industrial arts. "You don't just do the calculations and get out of it. Everything you do, you apply to something," Chounet said. "The old Voc Ed was, 'You come out of high school. You get a job.' Now, students learn skills they can use throughout their lives, in many different jobs."

Chounet also teaches at a local junior college and sees the difficulty some students have in making the transition to more advanced and technical courses. "A lot of times when you go from the high school to the junior college, nothing fits. We're trying to get a little bit of coordination between the two, especially in the technical areas."

Senior Shantelle Andrews has learned to apply her computing skills to interests in agriculture and business, as well as academics. She is up at 5:00 A.M. daily to feed and tend her herd of fifty Angus cattle, and back at 5:00 P.M. to do the same.

More Than a High School Library

The familiar hush of the library is punctuated by the tapping of keyboards as students type up reports and conduct research at a bank of computers. From a side room comes the voice of a teacher: "Now we move onto a different kind of operatic school, the German School." It is a music appreciation course being beamed in, via satellite, from Stanislaus College.

Ernie Wall calls the school's high-tech library "the focal point of everything around here in instruction." All incoming freshmen are required to take a six-week course on basic study skills, test-taking, and library skills, as well as state requirements for driver education and drug and alcohol awareness.

Wall emphasizes the importance of library skills because, he says, "Every teacher, every class, has something going on in the library." By the end of their freshman year, students are able to "help anybody who wanted to go in there and locate any piece of information."

With its satellite college courses, shelves well stocked with literature and reference books, and computers featuring encyclopedias on CD-ROM, the Dos Palos High School Library has become a valuable educational resource for the community. It also stays open four nights a week, something many of California's public libraries can no longer afford to do.

Faye Johnson notes with irony that some graduates return to the high school library because their college libraries no longer subscribe to publications still readily found on the shelves at Dos Palos.

In between, Andrews can be found reciting Shakespeare in her English class, completing equations in honors calculus, or logging in livestock stats on a Macintosh in the Ag building. As secretary of the school's chapter of Future Farmers of America, she keeps a spreadsheet on the status of livestock and crops for the group's 250 members.

When she described the new technology adopted during her four years at Dos Palos, she sounded more like the business

manager of a large organization than a high school senior. "We've really utilized our computers very well," she said. "My freshman year I came in and we didn't have anything. Everything was handwritten, there were papers everywhere, and it was so unorganized. I can't tell you how much everything has changed. Now I can go and pull anything up on the computer."

Andrews has also applied her expertise to the family business by computerizing farm accounts and setting up an inventory system for her mother's gift shop. As she finished her

Journalism students Fidelina Mendoza and Yolanda Ochoa founded La Ola Latina, the Spanish-language version of the school paper.

senior year and prepared to leave home for college, one of her tasks was teaching her mother how to use the technology. "The time we spend alone working on the computer lets me get closer to both my parents. It's helped them, and it helps me too because I learn a lot. It's a learning process all the way around."

Two enterprising Dos Palos journalism students, Fidelina Ochoa and Yolanda Ruiz, used their desktop publishing skills to produce a Spanish-language version of the school paper and a Spanish-language bulletin for parents to keep them informed of events at the school.

"It only took us one edition of the English newspaper to realize we wanted to do the Spanish newspaper," said Ochoa, who saw the frustration of classmates who couldn't read the school paper. "There were all these things going on at school they didn't know about, and it pertained to them too," said Ruiz. "They're part of the school."

La Ola Latina elicits a lot of response from the students. "They will write on the Spanish edition of the newspaper, hand it back to me, and say, 'Here, read my comments,'" said Ochoa, who was born in Mexico but schooled in the United States. In the process of producing the newspaper, she said, her Spanish has improved considerably. "We learned a lot. We're good with the accents now, and spelling and grammar."

Like many students at Dos Palos, the two juniors automatically assume college or occupational training will be the next step after graduation, and they have definite ideas about the future. "I'm going to be an art teacher," said Mendoza, showing off a fourteen-foot whale she crafted for the school's upcoming prom. Mendoza plans to major in psychology. "I hope I don't change my mind," she said. "It's better to have everything set."

In 1993, 80 percent of Dos Palos High School's graduating seniors were bound for college. The counseling staff began a long-range project tracking how many students stay in college, how long it takes them to get their degrees, and the employment history of those who enter the workforce. Similar surveys in the school's agriculture department in recent years have found nearly all of its graduates either in college or trade school or employed in agriculture or related fields.

Faye Johnson remembered a phenomenon that signaled a change in the number of minority students making college plans. "I saw the kids start wearing the USC hats and UCLA T-shirts," she said. "It's expected of them, and expected of themselves: you are going to go to college. I think that's a tremendous turnaround. It's coming from parents, it's coming from school."

Before becoming principal, Wall was a counselor at the school, and his strong emphasis on guidance is evident. Dos Palos counselors offer a number of incentives that encourage students to apply to college or trade schools. Financial-aid forms are distributed to all graduating seniors, registration for local colleges is held on the Dos Palos campus, and students are able to apply some course credits toward a college degree for a head start.

Wall cites collaboration and risk taking as the two essential elements contributing to the success of Dos Palos High School. "Those are probably the biggest things you'll find out here, compared to other schools," said Wall. "If you're afraid to take a risk, you're not going to get funded."

Over the years of seeking and administering grants and other supplemental funding, the Dos Palos educators discovered that the process can pose many new challenges. "A grant gives you the impetus and gives you outside validation that you've got the right idea," said Johnson. "To build on the opportunity, you need local support."

According to Johnson, for every grant dollar received Dos Palos High School puts in two local dollars. When the Apple grant was awarded, the school immediately set aside funds for additional Macintosh computers and for teacher training—a cost often overlooked by schools when adopting new technology. "We hear so much about the need for training, but so few of us actually treat it as the critical investment it truly is," Johnson said. "At Dos Palos, we view it as a cost of doing business, just like the electric bill."

In a subsequent grant proposal, Dos Palos administrators described how they had combined their Apple grant with local resources, a federal investment grant, and a state restructuring planning grant "to build the capacity for sweeping change."

Wall is aware of the risk of trying to do too much, and mindful of the careful balance that must be maintained to continue to "do what we're doing well." For him to achieve that requires a supportive and flexible teaching staff.

"We've been very creative, and we've been very conservative," said Johnson, describing some of the trade-offs teachers must make in exchange for technology and other improvements. "Several of our teachers teach seven periods a day, and they *all* teach six. That is not common in other schools."

A recent grant opportunity was passed up because Wall realized the staff was already under enough pressure to administer existing programs. "I said, 'Even though it's a good grant, none of us can take another grant like that. Let's just try to accomplish something here, rather than spread ourselves too thin.'"

The staff seems proud of the school's status as an innovator. "Our school is probably one of the most technically advanced in the state in terms of the number of computers per student," said Howard Lewis. "Ernie's been a really supportive force in terms of technology, and the teachers are becoming more and more comfortable using it."

"What's particularly impressive is most everyone here likes their job, likes what they're doing, and that's a big motivator," said Pierini. Wall is "not afraid to try things, and that's why we're really unique," she said. "Dos Palos is like a magnet."

Some school administrators, Johnson said, often "spend more time building their own kingdoms than building a kingdom for the kids." When push comes to shove, she added, our priorities go to the kids. "As long as that's what's happening in the school, then you're okay, and it's going to be okay for the kids. It doesn't mean we're not struggling. It's a question of priorities."

The school's philosophy was best stated in a grant proposal: "We have learned that 'technology plans' and advice about them abound, but it is people who make technology happen."

Computer Mini-School: Technology Builds Community

P.S. 125 Ralph Bunche School

New York, New York

There are few things in the world more rewarding than watching kids in the process of discovering and learning. That "aha!" when a student makes a connection is a wonderful sight, and our computer program has offered more than the average share of these moments.

Paul Reese,
COMPUTER MINI-SCHOOL

101

*J*ust before 8:00 A.M., nearly an hour before classes begin, they start filtering in: children wearing dark blue uniforms with an insignia bearing the name Ralph Bunche School. It is a public elementary school, with a sea of matching pleated skirts, slacks, and sweaters. But the room seems suddenly filled with an elite (if diminutive) corps.

The students rush to computer workstations and log on. It is a blustery, early winter morning in New York City, with freezing rain coming down in diagonal sheets. The windows of the fourth-floor corner room register the force of the storm, but all attention is focused inward. The kids from Harlem are calculating how close to Oregon they'll get in a covered wagon with a particular allotment of hay, flour, and sugar.

Paul Reese sits in front of his Macintosh at the head of several rows of Apple II and Macintosh computers. He sifts through volumes of electronic mail, trying to get a jump on the day as more kids fill the room.

There are messages from schools in Canada and Norway, notes from former students and colleagues, and inquiries from academics, researchers, and software companies. Reese's determination to dispense with these electronic missives is eventually thwarted by reality: he is even more in demand in person than he is on-line.

"You don't know what to do now? Go ahead, take the 'caps lock' off, I don't want it all in capital letters," he advises a third-grader working on an essay for the school newspaper. A nearby laser printer begins popping out multiple copies of someone's drawing. Reese checks the network on-screen, finds no clue as to the source of the abstract image, and the printer continues to churn it out.

Paul Reese's students access a variety of projects via the school server.

"In addition to being a teacher, and sort of the lead teacher in the computer school, I am the technical assistant, and the technical assistant to the assistant," explains Reese, the guiding force behind the Computer Mini-School at P.S. 125, also known as Ralph Bunche, in Central Harlem.

This school-within-a-school evolved out of a three-year experiment with Bank Street College researchers who were looking at ways to improve elementary science education through the use of local area networks. Now Reese and eight other teachers in grades three through six have incorporated the

In 1919, at the end of World War I, a new school was established in Central Harlem with great expectation. The Lincoln School on West 123rd Street in Central Harlem was a private, progressive, Dewey-inspired high school dedicated to educating young Rockefellers and other children of the elite.

In his memoir *Death Be Not Proud,* author John Gunther noted that his son, whose life and early death the book chronicles, had attended Lincoln School, "which he loved with all his heart."

In 1948 the building was sold to the City of New York, and the former Lincoln School became Public School 125. The name of statesman Ralph Bunche was added to the school's title in 1969, the result of a citywide initiative to give public schools an identity beyond their traditional numeric designation.

Bunche, the first African American to receive a Ph.D in political science, received the 1950 Nobel Peace Prize for his work in negotiating an end to the Arab-Israeli war of 1948. At the time, Bunche was principal secretary of the United Nations Palestine Commission. He had previously served as a division head in the U.S. Department of State. Bunche died in 1971.

Ralph Bunche School is bounded by disparate landmarks several blocks in each direction. To the west and south is Columbia University, whose closest satellite building is just two blocks from the school. Also nearby are Barnard College and the Union Theological Seminary.

West, toward the Hudson River, are Grant's Tomb and Riverside Church. To the north, and visible from some classrooms, is one of Harlem's most celebrated structures, the Apollo Theatre.

Half the classrooms of the Computer Mini-School face a massive skyline to the north: the nine brick buildings of the General Grant Houses, a public housing project that is home to many of the students of P.S. 125.

Across the street, on the south side of the school, is Morningside Park. In the 1960s, Columbia University proposed building a gymnasium on the park's hilly acreage, and the plan became the focus of a turbulent student protest. After a great deal of public outcry, the proposal was abandoned, and today the park forms the backdrop for Ralph Bunche's sister school for students in kindergarten through second grade.

technology across the entire curriculum, taking over a floor of the post–World War I brick building.

Reese had been a teacher here for more than a decade when the school purchased its first computer in 1980. A fourth-grade teacher with a specialty in math and science, he taught himself how to use the technology, started a computer club at the school, and eventually gave up his regular class to become the computer teacher. Now, he also serves as technical adviser for sixteen other schools in Community School District 5.

His career as an educator began directly out of college in the 1960s, in Rhodesia (now known as Zimbabwe) teaching secondary math and science for three years. On his return to the United States, and after a stint as a summer youth worker in East Harlem, Reese joined the Urban Teacher Corps and became a faculty member at P.S. 125, where he has remained for more than two decades.

In that time, the school has been honored with numerous corporate grants and awards and has gained a reputation for innovation among technologists and academics. In 1990, Reese was named *Electronic Learning* magazine's "Educator of the Year."

"There are few things in this world more rewarding than watching kids in the process of discovering and learning," he said. "That 'aha!' when a student makes a connection is a wonderful sight, and our computer program has offered more than the average share of these moments."

In 1987, when researchers from Bank Street College were looking for a location to conduct their studies on students and technology, they found a natural partner in Paul Reese and Ralph Bunche School. With support from the National Science

Foundation and twenty computers from Apple Education Grants, they installed an innovative computer network called Earth Lab. The objective was to see what would happen when grade-school students were given the same kind of communications tools that scientists use for collaborative study.

They chose weather patterns as the primary subject focus for the science curriculum and installed a weather station on the roof of the five-story building. A network was set up to enable students and teachers to call up common files and applications on any computer in the school and to communicate using electronic mail.

Students collected daily weather data, compiled it on a network database, and exchanged information and observa-

COMPUTERS IN THE CLASSROOM

tions electronically amongst themselves and with other schools. Herbert Williams, now a student at Bronx High School of Science and Technology, remembers the routine.

"Every morning we'd go up to the roof and take weather data. Then we'd go onto the computer and put that data into the database and keep a record of it, and use that information to compare and analyze. After a while we started to see patterns, and then," he recalled matter-of-factly, "we would be able to predict the weather."

When Hurricane Hugo began winding through the southern states in 1989, Earth Lab students used on-line weather data to predict its path—ahead of National Weather Service reports.

"The news was saying it was going to turn and go up the coast, and we were concerned it was coming to New York," Reese recalled. Students tapped into the raw weather data, which is updated hourly on CompuServe, and carefully plotted the path of the storm. It appeared to them that the hurricane would be moving back toward sea.

"We were almost uncomfortable with the data we had, because it contradicted what the news was saying," said Reese. As it turned out, the student forecasters were correct, and the hurricane bypassed New York.

Many Earth Lab students, including Williams, got an extra boost in mastering the technology through a computer home-loan program, which encouraged families to work together to learn computer skills. In one student's family, the program inspired a father to learn to read and subsequently return to school to pursue an education.

For Reese's students, the technology was also used to explore personal and emotional issues as well as science, math, and language. Reese related a story of two students, engaged in a dispute, who were asked to send "incident reports" to the teacher over the network. Ten minutes later the teacher found the two working at adjacent computers, carefully checking each other's versions, and essentially resolving the conflict. As a result of this episode, students who would otherwise be sent to the main office for discipline are now routinely asked to resolve their problems in electronic reports to their teachers.

Teachers involved in the Earth Lab project also began collaborating more and sharing information on the network. "I like the symbolic nature of computers and the ability to go with

COMPUTERS IN THE CLASSROOM

ideas no matter where they may be," said Reese, displaying a characteristic enthusiasm for technology's potential to transform learning.

At the conclusion of the three-year Earth Lab project in 1990, Reese and several colleagues developed a plan for a "computer mini-school." In part a response to persistent classroom problems, the plan proposed a reduction in class sizes, elimination of disruptive pull-out programs, and integration of technology across the entire curriculum.

After rather lengthy negotiations, the proposal for the mini-school was approved. Six teachers agreed to give up their contractual preparation periods in exchange for smaller class size; they then worked out ways to integrate remedial work and other mandated programs into their classroom routine. "When you talk about school restructuring, it's not just about the technology," said Reese. "Basically we created a community that's supportive—a common approach."

"When you have thirty-five kids in your room, you so much want to do your best, but you are juggling," said computer school teacher Kathy De la Garza, recalling her frustrations with the regular program before joining the mini-school. "You try to set up a routine, and it gets broken all the time. You have kids being pulled out for reading, pulled out for math, then the whole class is pulled out for science. It's just like a merry-go-round: it never stops."

Fifth-grade teacher Donna Stewart also found the realities of teaching in a traditional classroom different from what she had hoped. "Basically, I was a glorified baby-sitter," she said. "When you're in college, they don't tell you these things. They tell you that you're going to go in and essentially save the world. You're lucky if you can reach a few in the interim, because of the environment and what's happening. You try, and you do the best you can."

Stewart saw the mini-school, with its focus on technology and smaller class size, as an opportunity to "reach the children, teach them something that is going to help them in the future as far as modern technology, keep discipline problems at a minimum, and put into practice some of the things I had gone to college for."

With eight full-time teachers and two hundred students, the Computer Mini-School dominates one floor of classrooms. Each class spends two periods a week in the computer room

COMPUTERS IN THE CLASSROOM

on a variety of tasks: writing, working on spreadsheets, creating animations, or logging and editing videotape. Many students also gravitate back to the computer room before and after school and during lunch.

Several of the teachers also have computers in their classrooms, where students can work and transmit data over the network. Mona Monroe's sixth-graders use the classroom computer as a management tool. "The class itself has a class notebook," she said, describing her electronic ledger system. "Class officers have access to that notebook, which they jealously guard the password of—despite the fact that almost everybody at some time during the year gets to be a class officer and knows the password."

Her students use the electronic class notebook to manage their classroom in much the same way the school's office, or any business office, would. "If we collect money to go on a trip or to buy books for the book club, the treasurer keeps a record on the computer rather than a paper record," explained Monroe. "If we go on trips and the children bring permission slips, the class secretary makes a list that says who has brought their permission slip, and prints that out for the office the day we go on the trip."

Monroe, who has taught at Ralph Bunche since 1960, was the first teacher at the school to have a networked computer installed in her classroom. The class notebook was an idea she implemented during the first year of Earth Lab: "It's not teaching computers, not doing lessons on computers, and not doing school work, but it's a 'real work world' use of computers."

The mini-school's alternative approach to learning quickly proved its value in test scores, according to Assistant Principal John Diopoulos. "In the first year," he said, "the mini-school classes outperformed the regular school by almost 20 percent. The test results were remarkable, to say the least."

Diopoulos would like to see the program expanded if the school's physical structure could handle it; "I have more teachers who want to come in, but the problem becomes space." For every two classrooms that convert from the regular school, he explained, three classrooms are required to accommodate reduced class sizes.

"Right now we're at a critical stage where I can't add another classroom," he said. "I had to vacate a room because of water damage, and it takes forever to get things fixed. When they open up one problem, there's another problem behind it." As an example, it had been three years since the Earth Lab weather station was used because of damage to the school's roof.

Undeterred, students and teachers have pursued other forms of collaborative data collection, including a global "shadows" project. Students calculate the time of "solar noon" by taking sunrise and sunset data from the daily newspaper. At the appointed hour (assuming there is sunlight), they go to the schoolyard armed with a tripod and meterstick to measure their own shadows. Then they enter the collected data into a spreadsheet and forward it to other schools involved in the project, including sites in Boston, Australia, and Sweden.

"We're asking them to develop their own theories for the explanation of seasonal changes," said Reese. Weekly weather logs received from schools around the world also broaden the students' knowledge of geography and global weather patterns:

10/19-25/92

On Saturday evening, October 24, we had a time change. This shows up significantly in the time the sun rises and sets. The

weather was extremely nice for this week. Now the weather has changed! We have snow!

Maple Leaf School, Winnipeg, Manitoba, Canada

10/19-25/92

After warm weather in the beginning of October, very quick cooling snow almost reached Vienna. The mountains are sometimes not passable because of snowstorms.

Bundesgymnasium, Vienna, Austria

In addition to students and researchers from Columbia Teachers College and Bank Street College, Ralph Bunche School attracts a steady stream of visitors. Corporate executives, local dignitaries, congressional staffers, and even superstar athletes have all made the trip to the school on West 123rd Street.

Any encounter inside or outside the school becomes potential material for the student-produced newspaper and video news reports, including a visit by photographer Julie Chase for this book. Student Valerie Idehen wrote:

The kids in class 401 were showing Julie Chase and her assistant Ron [Schreier] their science projects. Many of the projects need-

ed the use of a flashlight. Julie took a picture of Isaiah Meek's science project, "How much rock can moving water carry?" and of Matrice Brown's project, "The earth is like an egg."

But I have one question for Matrice. Since the Earth is like an egg in many ways, will the earth crack? And does it have yolk inside?

Student reports have featured such notables as former Democratic Party national chair and commerce secretary Ron Brown, former Canadian prime minister Brian Mulroney, baseball star Darryl Strawberry, Olympic medalists Matt Biondi and Diane Dixon, and singer Julio Iglesias.

Production of the monthly newsletter, also under the direction of teacher Mona Monroe, is not unlike that in a professional newsroom. Fifth-grader Veronica Rivera described the process: "You write words, you save it. Later on, you go back and correct the mistakes. You do whatever you want." To submit your work for publication, she explained, you send it electronically to the newspaper's network address. Student editors then download the articles and decide which ones to publish.

Rivera and classmate Greg Streeter collaborated on a story about a class visit to Fraunces Tavern, a historic landmark on the city's downtown waterfront:

> On our trip, we had a tour guide that helped us around and told us about the different monuments inside the tavern. We did something special. Each of us were different people from the past. For example, Greg was a slave and Veronica was an insurance agent. Although we had fun, it was difficult to do.

Their story not only appeared in the Ralph Bunche *Computer School News,* but also in *This Week in AGE,* an international newsletter published by schools involved in the Apple Global Education project. Next to their story, on the front page, was a story about a ninth-grade Norwegian boy with AIDS. It described an informational meeting held at the boy's school in Norway:

> Finally Odd Kåre's mother stepped forward and told us about Odd Kåre, how he got the infection and about the bleeder illness. Then one person, Solveig from grade 9, stood up and said those words that she became famous for: "Go home and say good night to Odd Kåre from us. Tomorrow we will all meet him like a friend."

Ralph Bunche students also address issues of concern to their own neighborhood. Bulletin boards in the school hallways are decorated with colorful student artwork expressing messages such as "We Need Peace in Harlem East!" and "Stop the Violence: Love Each Other." Sixth-grader Renso Vasquez spoke at a school assembly, following an antiviolence march, and later published his speech in the school paper. It concluded with this passage:

A lot of bad people go around your neighborhood and they just come there just to be selling drugs or to rob a store. We can

"KidWitness News" is one of the innovative programs developed at Ralph Bunche School.

solve that problem by sending in more policemen and women. And the shootings? These can be stopped when the police arrest people selling guns because those guns are just like throwing your life away. These are my wishes and if they happen, this city would be safer for the children of the future.

Newsroom activity also involves the creation of video news reports for "KidWitness News," an educational initiative sponsored by Panasonic. Reports have ranged from interviews with local politicians and sanitation workers to coverage of the funeral mass for a popular school superintendent.

Students in the mini-school are selected from the student body by lottery, which, according to Assistant Principal Diopoulos, makes the mini-school "a true representation of the school as a whole."

"We really have a diversity of ability in our classrooms," confirmed teacher De la Garza. "I see children who come into my classroom who are at a lower level, and by the time they leave at the end of the year they know they're not. They have really pulled up because they see what's happening around

them. They see what other people are capable of doing; they push themselves more and they expect more of themselves."

Through Earth Lab and the mini-school, Ralph Bunche School has set a standard for the integration of technology in the classroom. But Reese believes the school "can't just live on its laurels." In that spirit, he has installed new networking technology to expand their telecommunications potential. Over one hundred students now have their own Internet addresses. "Earth Lab was designed to be a model for how kids would use electronic computers," said Reese. "I'm interested in making sure that that model is not a dead model." Only a few weeks after the students were up on the Internet, one of Reese's students had already exchanged several electronic messages with a correspondent at Penn State.

Two of his former students are assisting Reese in his quest to make the technology more relevant. Working after school and on weekends, Herbert Williams and Hamidou Diori maintain the network for Reese, doing everything from installing new equipment to compiling school attendance records.

"On Wednesdays, I help Mr. Reese with special network problems, because the networks have been going down and up," explained Diori, a 1992 Ralph Bunche graduate. "Something's wrong with our cabling on the Ethernet."

Diori also consults with the sixth-graders as a senior editor on the mini-school newspaper. After helping Reese install the Internet server four years ago, he wrote about the experience for his eighth-grade English class:

> I left my house knowing that I had enough skill to be able to assist my former teacher in helping him and a person from BBN [Bolt Beranek and Newman Inc., a high-tech company] support

Students use the Internet for research and to participate in on-line discussions on a variety of subjects.

staff, Susan Mills, in helping put up a network. This was no ordinary network, it was going to become a node on the Internet. . . . Mr. Reese gave me the okay to check the router. The leased line was not in yet but we still could connect via ordinary phone lines. . . . My job was to set up all the Macs that had hard drives with MacTCP, then configure their IP (Internet protocol) address, then configure the gateway address (the router). Finished that, no problem. Now to check it. Can I say it any better? It worked nicely.

"I like using telecommunications a lot, and especially on the Internet," said Diori. "When I get to one of these UNIX computers, I like messing around at the prompt, trying to find stuff." He subscribes to several "lists" on the Internet, where he engages in electronic discussions on a variety of subjects, including rap music, bicycles, and of course networking.

"I always wanted to learn to use computers," he said. His fascination with technology began in early childhood in Africa. He recalled that representatives from a computer company once came to his older sister's classroom in Nigeria to teach students how to use their system. "I always wanted to sneak in to see what they were doing, but they wouldn't let me in."

Once, while awaiting a flight in the West African country of Ivory Coast, his mother got permission for him to tour the airport's computer system. When he typed his name on a keyboard and saw it come up on the monitor, he was mesmerized. "It was such a little thing, but I was so excited about it," he said.

In 1989, he and his family emigrated from Nigeria, landing in the Central Harlem neighborhood of predominantly African American, Hispanic, and Caribbean residents. The young computer fan got a lucky break when he enrolled at his neighborhood school: "The first day I came into the computer room I was so surprised. I saw all these kids on computers and I said, 'Wow, kids actually get to use computers over here.'"

Now he regularly scans computer bulletin boards and on-line services to find such items as the "top ten" music list for his sister and a new disk drive for his mother. He added: "I keep in contact with Mr. Reese on the Internet."

He described finding articles on the subject of recycling for a HyperCard stack he was creating for his seventh-grade Earth Sciences class. Using the Wide Area Information Service, he first typed in *recycling*. "It gave me a directory of servers on the Internet that have articles on recycling or have *recycling* in the database. I typed in *recycling* a second time, and I got the actual article—and it was all real-time."

The HyperCard stack will also incorporate a QuickTime video clip from an interview Diori did on the subject of recycling while still a student at P.S. 125. "I'm going to upload it to various BBSs [bulletin board systems] when I'm done, so that people can look at it," he said.

Since leaving Ralph Bunche School, Herbert Williams repeatedly found himself in a quandary that may be common to other graduates of Reese's computer program: he was overqualified for most computer classes offered at the junior high school and high school level.

In his first year at the Bronx High School for Science and Technology, Williams was allowed to waive the required freshman computer literacy course after taking a skills test. The computer coordinator asked if he would like to take a course in the BASIC programming language instead, but he already knew BASIC. The only course left was telecommunications—a class reserved for seniors. As the only freshman in the class he felt slightly out of place, but he "got used to it." By the end of that first year, he had completed the school's computer science curriculum.

Now, most of his time on the computer is spent at the Ralph Bunche mini-school, or at his job with a children's rights organization called Kids Meeting Kids. For this group, among other tasks, he helps administer an electronic conference about children's rights on the PeaceNet, "sharing information about what's happening to children around the world, and what young people and adults can do to help."

Ellen Clare

"That woman who was in here yelling at me, which she does all the time, keeps me in line and honest," said Paul Reese about Ellen Clare, a thirty-five-year veteran of P.S. 125, who seems to have the same effect on her students.

When you encounter her class of twenty-two fourth-graders in the hall, you can hear a pin drop. Although she is lagging behind and out of view, they wait for her obediently, all lined up in their neat blue uniforms according to height.

As she comes down the corridor on this wintry Friday, her tall, black, reed-thin frame is decked out in cowboy boots, long narrow blue jeans, and a blue velour top. Her hair is cropped close to the head, and a single sterling silver pendant hangs from her neck. Her bearing is regal and stylish. She peers at her charges through oversized spectacles, and only when she gives the word do they march.

In the classroom, she emotes an uncanny blend of fire, brimstone, and humor. The children are, to use one of Clare's fourth-grade vocabulary words, "mesmerized"—although some might argue that "terrorized" is more like it.

Her traditional teaching style was even the subject of an editorial in the school newspaper under the title "Is Mrs. Clare a Great Teacher?" Student Edward Velasquez wrote, "The children think that Mrs. Clare is mean. So I inter-

With two years of high school left to go, his goals for college are remarkably clear: a double major in journalism and psychology. He already contributes to special electronic forums for writers.

If those plans change, he said, he'll always have computing to fall back on. "In the future, every career is going to involve a computer," he said, adding that students who don't have the opportunity to develop good computer and keyboard skills will be missing out. "It's a really useful tool, and soon it's just going to be within all our lives."

viewed Mrs. Clare. Mrs. Clare likes being a teacher because she wants to make sure that the children will get a good education so they can meet their needs when they are adults."

Ellen Clare surprised some colleagues when she became a member of the Computer Mini-School in 1992. Assistant Principal John Diopoulos did not expect one of the school's staunchest traditionalists to embrace the mini-school concept, but, he admitted, "even the senior teachers see the benefits, because they get so much done." While noting that Clare is still relatively computer-phobic, Reese has high praise for her contribution to the mini-school, saying simply, "She's marvelous."

In her classroom, that delicate balance of discipline and whimsy is reflected in the attentiveness and enthusiasm of her students. In a discussion of the book *The Witches,* students are eager to be called on to read and explain parts of the story. They speak loudly, and slowly, sounding out the syllables.

"This is much more than a job," Clare said, citing the many long afternoons and Saturdays spent there. "Many of my students have a lot of anger. They don't really know they can do this."

It's Clare's job to tell them they can.

When Williams returns to Ralph Bunche School and sees what the younger students are doing, he is impressed. "It's a lot of fun to see what the people after me are doing. They do a lot of work, even the third graders—a lot of work." Williams believes many of them know more about technology than most computer professionals, and he gives Paul Reese a lot of credit: "He had a lot of projects that helped us."

JoAnne Kleifgen, a faculty member at Columbia Teachers College and director of a bilingual teaching project at Ralph Bunche for Spanish-speaking and Haitian students, reaffirmed the value of the Computer Mini-School approach. "My students and I have volunteered a lot because we are learning. It's not just out of the goodness of our hearts. We're learning from Paul, and from the kids, and the teachers."

"To me, and a whole lot of kids here, school is like a home," said Journelle Clark, a student in Doris Parker's sixth-grade class. "The teachers are very good at trying their best to provide the best for the kids."

Reese adds: "We have a lot of kids who do not have any order in their life, and some of them very much need a clear sense of order. I don't mean a repressive order, but I mean a predictable, reliable source of routine and limits."

Computer Mini-School newcomer but longtime Ralph Bunche teacher Ellen Clare considers herself "one of the luckiest people in the world" to be part of the program. She described a difficult, chronically defiant student who, toward the end of the term, scored at the top of the class. "That face," she said, remembering his reaction, "is worth ten salaries."

For Reese, the rewards are also intangible. "Clearly, I get a lot out of it. I enjoy working with the kids, I like the world of ideas," and the mini-school, he said, gives him the opportunity to explore that world.

Reese quickly shifted away from a discussion about teaching to eagerly return to the work at hand. "This week there's pressure to get the newspaper out," he said, listing several other projects including an upcoming video competition and a classroom greenhouse that are currently demanding his attention. "Some day I have to take care of the paperwork in here," he sighed, gesturing toward a cluttered corner of the room, "and . . . uh . . . clean my desk." But for Reese and his colleagues, the students obviously come first.

"It takes a special type of teacher," Diopoulos said, reflecting on the success of the Computer Mini-School. "I've been to a number of different schools at different times in my career; this works because of the staff."

Herbert Williams testified to the power of such care and dedication with a simple declaration: "I'll never forget what happened there."

CHAPTER 6

Myths and Legends: Creating New Traditions

Pine Ridge High School

Pine Ridge Indian Reservation, South Dakota

You've got a long, long future ahead of you, but you've got to have education, and you've got to keep the culture with it. Don't leave the culture behind.

> Oliver Red Cloud
> CHIEF OF THE LAKOTA SIOUX

*I*t was 6:00 A.M. and still dark as Tom Gray pulled away from his cabin on the South Dakota prairie. A jackrabbit jumped into the headlights and sprinted along the snow-covered road, comfortably ahead of the truck. "He's leading the way," Gray said with a smile, beginning the one-hour trip to Pine Ridge School. Half way there, Gray pointed toward the rising sun and a sign reading "Now Entering the Pine Ridge Indian Reservation." "When you pass that fence," he said, "you're in another country."

On this crisp January morning, Gray parked his truck in front of a two-story brick building at Pine Ridge High School and climbed the stairs to a corner classroom. With framed artwork on the walls, a coffee machine in one corner, and several computers on each of the tables, it appeared more like a casual work area. A little after 7:00 A.M., several students came in and quietly got to work, designing and printing up a program for an assembly that was to take place that morning.

In the school's main office, a radio on top of the filing cabinet crackled with a live report of Bill Clinton's inauguration as president of the United States. The broadcast was barely audible above the noise of a nearby copy machine; the event went virtually unnoticed and unremarked.

High school students soon began to fill the bleachers in the school's gymnasium for a different kind of ritual, one with more immediate significance for the staff and students of Pine Ridge. It was a traditional "Wiping of Tears" ceremony to honor a beloved teacher, Harvey Nelson, who had died of a heart attack exactly one year before at age forty-six. Gray's students handed out copies of the program as their classmates gathered to mark the end of the traditional period of mourning.

While Maya Angelou stood on the steps of the Capitol in Washington, D.C., reciting her epic poem and referring to "the African and Native American, the Sioux," Chief Oliver Red Cloud, namesake and descendant of one of the most powerful Sioux war chiefs, reminded Pine Ridge students of the importance of education and of maintaining their cultural heritage—including the rituals surrounding death.

In the old days, Red Cloud explained, mourners would "stay away from everything for one year, cut their hair, stay away in the hills." Today, he said, some traditions have been lost. "In the white man's world it's different. Lakota life is hard. Then again, Wasicu* life is hard. We're in between."

Harvey Nelson, he said, was one of those teachers who "believed in the Lakota way," although he himself was not Indian. "We have teachers. They've been working hard, really working hard to teach you. On the other side we have Lakota people to teach the way," he said. "You've got a long, long future ahead of you, but you've got to have education, and you've got to keep the culture with it. Don't leave the culture behind. Try to keep it. Try to talk Indian."

As he spoke to the students, Red Cloud was engaged in an ancient Lakota custom. Through the centuries, storytelling has been the primary form of communication for the Lakota, ensuring the survival of their tribal traditions.

A Lakota prophesy holds that in the seventh generation after the 1890 massacre at nearby Wounded Knee Creek, the spiritual knowledge that was lost there would return. In front of a large mural depicting tribal legends, Chief Red Cloud reminded the students seated in the gymnasium of their place in history. "I'm standing here as chief of the Lakota Sioux tribe, fourth generation," he said. "You're the seventh generation here. You have to honor and respect yourselves." Gesturing to the table where a feather, pipe, tobacco, and other sacred items were spread, he said, "Someday one of you is going to do this—what we're going to show you and teach you."

---

*Wasicu ("wa-shee-chu") is a Lakota term for white culture. The literal translation, "to get bacon," comes from early trading days.

The school's Lakota Studies teacher, Warfield Moose, later talked about the importance of handing down stories. "For everything in our culture, the process of learning is reflected in oral tradition. We need to keep this alive, pass it on to a younger group, and hope they'll pick it up. This is how the Lakota oral tradition evolved all these years."

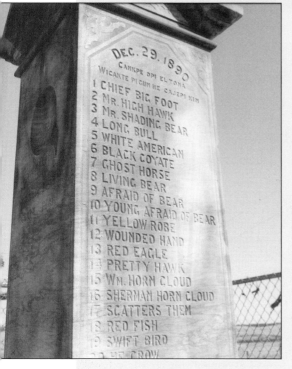

Not far from the community of Pine Ridge is Wounded Knee Creek, the site of the December 1890 Indian massacre that historian Dee Brown called "the symbolic end of Indian freedom." Among the three hundred Lakota killed and buried there in a mass grave were many women, children, and elders, including the revered Chief Big Foot.

The battle at Wounded Knee and the Ghost Dance religion* that prompted it are frequent subjects in Native American history classes at Pine Ridge High School. After teacher Bryan Brewer and several students visited the site, they talked of the tragedy. "It's kind of sad going there," said sophomore Seneca DeCory. "Kind of hard. If you watch those old movies, it just gets you mad. It shows all these people taking advantage of the Indians." After a moment he added, "But it's all in the past. After a while, you kind of forgive and forget."

Red Cloud and Moose both spoke to the students in the Lakota language. A Lakota elder brushed an eagle feather against the cheek of Harvey Nelson's widow, Joan, to signify the wiping away of tears. In the background, a circle of drummers beat out a mournful rhythm.

---

*The Ghost Dance movement expressed a desperate longing for restoration of the past—a return to life free of war, hunger, and disease—that accompanied the Lakotas' subjugation by whites.

Student Jonna Swiftwater recited a poem she had written in Nelson's honor and talked about the importance of the ritual. "Mr. Red Cloud has said before that this way has been done many times. This way is the old way, and it is up to us to keep this way sacred, and we must keep it going," she said.

At the end of the last "honoring song," the students formed a circle and filed past Joan Nelson to shake her hand and offer condolences.

The site of controversy and conflict for over a century, the Pine Ridge Reservation is the largest remnant of Sioux homelands that once included the Badlands, the Black Hills, and sizeable parts of Montana and Wyoming. After gold was discovered in the Black Hills at the end of the nineteenth century, government surveyors carved out new reservation boundaries. The land they chose for the Oglala Sioux was a fraction of their former territory, and considered nearly worthless. Even so, at 4,590 square miles, Pine Ridge is the second largest reservation in the United States.

Gerald Ray, seen here talking with students, is principal of the upper division at Pine Ridge High School.

COMPUTERS IN THE CLASSROOM

The legacy of betrayal, broken promises, and brutality still haunts the reservation's fifteen thousand residents, descendants of a people who once roamed the western prairies and mountains. Many count among their ancestors the victims and survivors of the 1890 massacre at Wounded Knee, the last major battle between federal troops and American Indians.

The Pine Ridge Reservation has the highest poverty level in the country, with over 70 percent unemployment and few economic opportunities. The impact on reservation children was described in Pine Ridge school's 1991 grant proposal to Apple Computer:

> The students at Pine Ridge come from a closed and isolated community environment. Few students have experience with or exposure to any type of culture or belief other than the Lakota family unit.... The community does not support a library, youth programs, or recreational activities.... Reading scores average three to five years below grade level.

The school is located in the community of Pine Ridge, where about one-third of all reservation residents live. The campus is divided into primary and secondary levels for students from kindergarten through high school. It is one of the few remaining government-run boarding schools for Native American students, with about 250 of the 700 students living in dormitories on campus during the week. Many other students who live in remote parts of the reservation travel long distances each day to school.

Reservation schools have always had an uneasy and ill-defined charter, a legacy of the nineteenth-century practice of sending Indian children to distant boarding schools with the promise that they would learn valuable skills and later return

Tom Gray played a key role in developing the Myths and Legends program, which uses computer technology to incorporate Oglala Sioux traditions into the school curriculum.

to help their families. At many of these schools the children were given new names and uniforms, had their hair cut, and, in a final attempt to wipe out all remnants of Indian culture, were forbidden to speak their native language. One former student of a reservation school in the 1930s recalled having the language literally beaten out of him, returning to his family to find that he could no longer communicate with them.

Bryan Brewer, now a Native American Studies teacher at Pine Ridge High School, remembers that as a student at the school in the 1960s, he and his classmates were punished for

Excerpt from "Shape-Shifter"

The Lakota culture, religion, and my ancestors fill me with pride. Yesterday, I saw our religion fading like steam from boiling water. Now, I see it coming back strong. I used to think I didn't need my religion or my culture but my grandmother changed everything. Mrs. Fast Wolf, my grandmother, told me I would feel a deep loss later in life and I would be weak to the negatives in life. She also said every Lakota woman needs to find her inner self. Grandmother Fast Wolf told me many stories of a long time ago when the Sioux and other tribes had to fight even to death for the use of what we believe in. I include myself in every Indian subject.

JAMIE FAST WOLF

speaking the Lakota language. Only in recent years has Native American culture been officially incorporated into teaching curricula.

Early in his tenure at Pine Ridge High School, English teacher Tom Gray, who is not Native American, saw how Lakota history and traditions could provide both an incentive for learning among his students and a powerful source for increased self-esteem. In addition to learning French or German, they could learn the Lakota language. He was impressed by the beauty and sophistication of traditional Lakota tales, and he began looking for new ways to incorporate them into his teaching.

Gray's interest in Native American culture was first sparked in 1983 during a visit to India as a member of a Rotary Club study exchange. When his Hindu hosts were told of his origins in South Dakota and Nebraska, he was asked repeatedly about life on the Indian reservations. "I didn't have a clue," Gray recalled.

His own grandparents were homesteaders on the western plains, selling bib overalls to sheepherders from the back of a wagon. Gray had heard "all the horror stories" about life on the reservations, but on his return from India he began to study the history of the area from a different perspective. A high school teacher across the border in Nebraska, he soon applied for and got a position teaching Title 1 remedial English at Pine Ridge High School.

For the next seven years, Gray immersed himself in a culture that for the first three decades of his life he knew little about—despite growing up just a few miles from the tribal headquarters of the Lakota nation. His fascination with Native American folklore led him to develop a theory about common myths and legends from around the world. When one of his students came to him for ideas for a research paper, he suggested she compare a common Sioux tale with a Greek myth containing similar elements.

"I said, 'Why don't you do something with the myth of Penelope, and the legend of the woman, blanket, and dog?,'" Gray recalled. A familiar Lakota legend tells of a woman sitting on the edge of the Badlands weaving a blanket. Every time she falls asleep, her dog unravels the blanket, and in the morning she must start all over again. The legend holds that if the woman were to finish the blanket, the world would end.

In the Greek myth, Penelope is pursued by a drunken band of suitors who believe her husband, Odysseus, is dead. She tells them that when she has finished weaving a special garment she will consent to marriage to one of them. Each night, after weaving all day, she unravels her work.

"The intercultural myth program started with this," Gray recalled. His students began to compare number systems, colors, and similar geometric patterns, such as the Stonehenge circle and the ancient tepee circles of the Lakota.

At the same time, Gray was becoming captivated by computer technology. He attended a conference on educational technology and saw a simple HyperCard animation that sparked his imagination. Designed by a student, the animation depicted the figure of a golfer. When a button on the screen was clicked, the golfer hit the ball. "I thought, 'I've got to do that. If these kids can do this in California, our kids can.'"

Like many schools operated by the Bureau of Indian Affairs, Pine Ridge lacked standard teaching tools and had only a couple of computers to share among all grade levels. A survey of the library revealed few new books, with many dating back to the 1930s—a time when some of the brick buildings on campus were still new. In addition to the lack of books and supplies, academic programs at reservation schools tended to reflect a bureaucratic "one size fits all" approach, with few attempts to adapt to the needs of a particular culture or community.

Gray imagined his students, many of whom demonstrated extraordinary artistic ability, using computers to illustrate and animate the stories and legends of their ancestors taken from interviews with tribal elders. He began to develop a curriculum that would focus on other cultures and disciplines as a bridge to the students' own cultural heritage.

With help from colleagues and school administrators, he put together a grant proposal to Apple based on a cross-cultural and interdisciplinary curriculum called Myths and Legends. A primary goal of the initiative was to link the traditions of the Oglala Sioux directly to the school curriculum, with the help of computers. The proposal noted that "most families do fos-

ter a belief and importance in their culture, and these traditions remain as the only common link between home and school, and therefore the world." Such an approach, they hoped, would provide an opportunity for parents and students to view the school "as an integral part of their lives," possibly for the first time.

The Apple grant was approved, and six new Macintosh computers were delivered to the school. The students were soon writing, illustrating, animating, and publishing on the computer. One talented student, Jamie Fast Wolf, quickly amassed hundreds of HyperCard stacks and illustrations of traditional stories and incidents in Lakota history. For example, in the legend of the Devil's Tower, two boys are saved from a mighty bear when the earth beneath them rises up to form a tower of solid rock. In Fast Wolf's depiction of the story, HyperCard enabled her to animate the motion of the earth.

"They had never seen something they'd drawn move!" said Gray. "It was revolutionary. There is no way you can describe what happens to the students when you start to see success like this."

The Myths and Legends curriculum inspired staged dramas interpreting Lakota legends. It culminated each semester with the publication of an anthology of student stories, poems, and illustrations called *Sparkling Silence.*

A year later, the school received a supplemental grant of twenty computers. While continuing their focus on Lakota culture, the students began to expand their use of the technology by composing and sampling electronic music and by filming and editing QuickTime videos.

Gray and his colleagues also began to apply the technology to other core subjects, including mathematics, where students used specialized applications to study everything from whole number skills to precalculus and trigonometry. "You have to link what they know to what they're going to have to know when they go out in the world," said Gray. "That's the paradox. You have to prepare them for the change factor. It's a hard job."

Within a short time the teachers and students of Pine Ridge had discovered a powerful new medium for creative expression and learning, well beyond the realm of drill and

practice. Balancing elements of native culture and new technology, they were exploring their own history.

"Quite honestly, there isn't a day goes by I don't walk in that room and I'm awed," said Gray, whose enthusiasm has had an influence on both students and teachers. "The kids have taught me as much as I've taught them."

For student Elmarla Little Spotted Horse, computers had held a fascination since elementary school. In the fourth grade, she remembered, the applications available at the time left her wanting more. "I thought, 'Wouldn't it be great if you could move a pencil around and make pictures (on the screen), instead of giving instructions and having the computer do it?'"

Through the Apple grant program, Little Spotted Horse learned how to script in HyperCard and began illustrating her stories with complex images and animations. "It made me wonder, what more can they do? What else do computers have to offer? How can we manipulate them to get what we're looking for?"

The Myths and Legends program, she said, was "the most meaningful part of high school," both for the access it gave her to technology and for the focus on Lakota history. "I learned a lot more about myself as an Oglala Sioux than I knew before," she said. "I didn't think much of the reservation because of what I saw on TV." Now a graduate of Pine Ridge, she has gone on to study computer graphics at the Denver Institute of Technology.

Seneca DeCory, a sophomore at the school, started out creating HyperCard stacks, then moved on to experiment with professional production software including MacroMind Director, SoundPro Edit, and Adobe Premiere. His favorite medium, though, is still HyperCard. "Everything else is too easy," he said. "I like the scripting, where I have to actually write the script down into computer language."

He applied his own musical skills to the soundtrack of an animated HyperCard stack that depicts a street musician playing a saxophone. "It's actually me playing it," he revealed. Another stack combines video footage of his older brother playing basketball with an illustrated animation that mirrors the same action. A stack in progress will feature video footage from a powwow where he participated as a drummer.

Like Elmarla Little Spotted Horse, DeCory's hopes for the future are tied to his new technology skills. "I hope to get a computer scholarship somewhere, or go into the Navy, where they use a lot of computers," he said.

The level of student involvement is remarkable when considered against the backdrop of past problems at the school. In the 1980s, Principal Imogene Horse recalled, students seemed to come to school only "for the social life." The school suffered from a terrible discipline problem, and Pine Ridge students regularly ranked at the bottom in regional exams. The teachers, she said, suffered from a lack of motivation. "They were so demoralized. They would lock their doors to eat."

Among the isolationists was the late Harvey Nelson. When Tom Gray first came to Pine Ridge, Nelson had been a fixture there for many years. He knew the people and the politics and had an understanding of and reverence for Lakota culture and traditions. But, according to his friends and family, teaching had become a tiresome routine.

Several things began to change his perspective. One was the school's revision of the entire K–12 curriculum, encouraging more coordination between teachers. "We realized that the thing we had to do was look at what was happening in the classroom," said Horse. "Nobody had been paying attention, really. Everybody was doing their own thing. You had no continuity. You'd hire a teacher, put them in, close the door, and that's about all."

But the change that had the biggest impact on Nelson was the introduction of new technology. In the few years they

Elmarla Little Spotted Horse (on right).

spent as colleagues and best friends, Gray and Nelson shared an enthusiasm about computers and their ability to transform education. "I don't know how you can get paid for having so much danged fun," Gray said. Both returned from a technology conference on the day before Nelson died.

"In my wildest expectation I would not have dreamed our students would be as interested and involved as they have been," said Horse. "We've changed more than I ever thought we could. The kids just behave beautifully. I wouldn't have believed that could happen for anything."

Gerald Ray, principal of the school's upper division, noted how changes at the school had influenced overall student scholarship. In local academic competitions, he said, Pine Ridge often used to place last. In recent years, however, his students have placed among the top five schools. "Scores are up," he said. "The school, I feel, is progressing. Computers have tied into it very well."

One of the most successful parts of the new computer-based curriculum was the establishment of telecommunication links with other Apple grantees, notably Edgewater High School in Orlando, Florida.

Students in Gene Bias's English class at Edgewater were not satisfied with the few references to Native Americans found in their standard high school texts. Teacher Chris Carey, the school's Apple grant coordinator, put Bias in touch with Tom Gray. Bias was impressed with examples of Pine Ridge student work, and Bias and Gray agreed to start an electronic information exchange program between their students.

Students at both sites created biographies of themselves on HyperCard, complete with scanned-in photographs resembling an electronic yearbook. "It was just like when you're young and interact with your pen pals," Little Spotted Horse recalled, "but when you send them pictures and letters, you do it through the computer using electronic mail."

The differences between the two regions are vast, geographically and ethnically. Edgewater is located in Orlando, one of the most popular year-round tourist destinations in the country. Although the student body represents a wide variety of ethnic origins, there are no Native American students. Pine Ridge, with its remote landscape and unique cultural environment, provided a stark contrast.

"When Tom and I set this thing up, our kids were so excited," said Bias. "I had nine different nationalities in my junior English class. They were on AppleLink almost every day." The process of learning about Pine Ridge, Bias said, inspired them to put together a multicultural Myths and Legends class of their own. "The kids, in essence, have been helping me write the curriculum."

Bias notes that many class assignments, such as writing to pen pals or interviewing and transcribing the histories of community elders, are not new activities. "What is new about it," he said, "is the way they're sharing this information through telecommunications."

He admits that once his students pick up on the technology, they tend to leave him in the dust. "There's a difference between teaching kids and doing it yourself," he said. "We don't tell them there is a fairly high learning curve. We just put them on the software, and they do it." Bias acknowledges that Tom Gray showed him that any student could master the technology: "That probably influenced me most and changed my thinking about technology. The more our kids get involved, the more they pull other teachers in."

Students share information through electronic exchange programs including AppleLink, ENAN (Educational Native American Network), NativeNet, and the Internet. "It gets kids prepared. It gives them a whole world they can share with." And, Bias added, it bolsters self-esteem. "To me, that's one of the biggest things."

Students from Edgewater and Pine Ridge also produced videos on each region, learning how to edit videotape on the computer. In Gray's classroom at Pine Ridge, student Eli Battese recorded an improvised flute melody into a microphone attached to the computer as he watched video clips move across the Macintosh screen. He was laying down a soundtrack for a QuickTime movie students had assembled that featured the rolling South Dakota hills, roaming buffalo, and other views of the local landscape.

As a result of their experiments with a variety of media, Bias initiated a multimedia production class at his school, and Gray and Bias created a demonstration CD-ROM containing student work from both schools.

After helping to bring new technology and new methods of teaching to Pine Ridge, Gray now spends time traveling to other Native American schools around the country, giving workshops to help teachers and students in remote locations tap into the information revolution.

At Takini, another Indian school in eastern South Dakota, Gray gave a seminar on HyperCard that, according to a staff member, "literally captivated all students." Gray introduced each class in school to the capabilities of HyperCard. At the end of the day, Gray later reported, "all the grades from K–12 wanted to start a new class with HyperCard as the focus, each promised to link me through telecommunications, and the seniors even shook my hand before they left for their next class."

After Gray's departure from Pine Ridge in 1993, students and teachers continued to explore the technology. Teacher Warfield Moose worked with senior Jonna Swiftwater to create a dictionary of Lakota terms on HyperCard, complete with

voice recordings. As part of an ongoing project, they have also begun to create an illustrated database of sacred objects.

Teachers Cliff DeLong, Bill O'Connell, and Randy Pence help students apply their technology skills to a wide range of class assignments, with Pence requiring students in his senior

English class to produce HyperCard illustrations for their term papers. Swiftwater chose to depict the changing face of life on the plains for her paper "The Oglala Sioux and White Society." In one animated sequence, a settlement of tepees gradually transforms into houses.

"That girl can do amazing things on the computer," said Moose. Swiftwater admits she's "falling in love with computers" and plans to pursue studies in technology and psychology at the University of South Dakota. For the summer following graduation, however, she will return to Pine Ridge school to work with Moose on a Lakota language and culture project based on HyperCard.

Swiftwater is determined to continue the work of documenting her culture in a medium that will help other students grasp the richness of their Lakota heritage. Her hope is to return to the school someday to train other students.

"I'm proud to be living on the reservation," she said. "I think we're special. Probably because I'm Indian, but still, I think we're special. We've had a lot happen to us, and to the land, but we're still living and we're still functioning in today's world. We're strong." It appears that at Pine Ridge, the members of the seventh generation are well on their way to fulfilling the prophesy of renewal.

As DeCory reflected on the history of Wounded Knee, he suddenly formulated an idea for a multimedia presentation. He could digitize clips from movies featuring stereotyped images of Indians, he said, and add his own commentary on racism. "We've got the equipment to do it, too," he said confidently.

In a story handed down through generations, a survivor of the battle had a vision: seven generations after the massacre the end of mourning would come, and a resurgence of Lakota culture and spirituality would begin. Many Lakota believe the current generation is representative of that new spirit. Brewer has high hopes for the "new group coming up," a younger generation of Lakota with a restored sense of pride and purpose.

Conclusion: Lessons Learned

*T*hrough its Education Grants program, Apple has attempted to identify key issues in education and ways technology can help address those issues. For nearly two decades, we at Apple have amassed a great deal of experience. Through this experience and the stories told in this book, we hope to provide valuable insight and lessons for the benefit of educators, policymakers, funders, and others who share our commitment to making a difference in schools and in the broader society.

The lessons the educators in this book have taught us help focus our attention on a holistic approach to solving important social, cultural, pedagogical, and economic problems that confront educators on a daily basis. There is no one recipe for success; what works for one school or district may not work for another. As the educators in this book reveal, the environment, resources, and people contribute to a unique blend of opportunities and circumstances that help guide vision and implementation. But what does connect the schools profiled in this book and many others with whom we've worked is a common set of beliefs and strategies that transcend the boundaries of geography, demography, and time and help create a framework for practical application in new settings.

To begin with, teachers embrace the belief that all children can learn. Armed with this belief, they seek new strategies for teaching to address a variety of learning styles and student interests. The definition of basic skills is broadened to include problem solving, critical thinking, and hypothesis testing. Learning across grade levels and subject matter is emphasized, requiring teachers to regularly collaborate on curriculum, outcomes, and evaluation measures. There is a paradigm shift from lone teacher as lecturer to teacher as facilitator and interdisciplinary team member. Students are no longer passive listeners. They actively guide classroom learning and inquiry. Computers are part of an overall strategy designed to help facilitate change and help create dynamic learning environments where students help construct knowledge. With computers, students can take greater control over their learning. They are able to take risks in problem solving, engage in computer-generated simulations and experiments, exhibit understanding through creation of multimedia products, visualize abstract concepts, and conduct independent and collaborative research using electronic communications. Teachers use computers to organize and plan curricula and collaborate with other educators on a variety of different issues using electronic communication.

In the schools profiled in this book, educators are attempting to create a seamless environment where students are empowered to make choices about the various technology tools and strategies available to get work done. Schools moving in this direction provide great models for preservice teachers and others who wish to learn from the experience.

Educators tell us that creating exceptional learning opportunities for their students as well as a change in delivery of instruction requires following a path that involves various stages of disequilibrium, reflection, and continuous improvement.

An essential first step in the process is to have a common vision of where you want to be. Getting there requires planning and flexibility. As we chronicle the achievements of educators in this book, we realize that they all sought to motivate students by making learning relevant and fun. Teachers, for the most part, initially took on what they thought would be manageable projects, working with small groups of students, focusing on one grade level as with the St. Benedict's team, or targeting a specific knowledge base such as science in the case of Ralph Bunche elementary and South Philadelphia High School. Careful introspection enabled teachers to question old practices and seek new ways of teaching to spark interest and raise the level of achievement in core subject areas.

Teachers recognized that for students to participate fully, they had to design strategies that would enable students to contribute their own unique cultural backgrounds and perspectives. Plans were structured to allow students to help invent curriculum frameworks based on their individual needs and interests. At Pine Ridge High School and Abita Springs Elementary School, this meant that students would help construct course content in social studies, history, and English by generating work based on authentic life experiences. This strategy instilled a sense of pride and confidence and led to new pathways of opportunity. Students saw themselves as experts; they conducted independent research and used multimedia to exhibit and illustrate their understandings and talents. Computer technology set no boundaries for students in Pine Ridge, who were able to travel in cyberspace, meet new students across the country, and provide content for a course on Native American Myths and Legends at Edgewater High School in Florida. Students were able to see their place and value in history.

In addition to making learning fun and relevant, educators at Dos Palos High School also took a more pragmatic approach to crafting a vision and developing a plan. The combination of a poor local economy and dwindling state funds threatened any innovation the school might want to try. Rather than seeking a quick fix to the problem, the school embarked on a comprehensive schoolwide restructuring mission. Both administrators and teachers took a global view of the marketplace with an eye toward the future. They set high standards of achievement for all students. All students would graduate, go to college, or—at the very least—leave school with requisite skills to prepare them for an increasingly competitive and technological workplace. Teachers would benefit from staff development. Courses were revised that integrated technology across all curriculum, all grade levels, and for all children. Student portfolios would serve as a new measure of assessing student performance. This type of comprehensive approach enabled the school to say no to potentially enticing grant opportunities that did not fit the school's overall vision and mission. Given constraints of time and resources, the school was able to set priorities to avoid fragmented approaches that could potentially derail the restructuring effort. Instead, Dos Palos High School established itself as a community learning center for residents and businesses, with its state-of-the-art library, satellite capability, and students willing to do real work for local businesses and civic organizations.

Other schools extended the boundaries of learning beyond the classroom, involving others in their effort. Their strategies involved partnerships with families and visiting artists to provide technical support and help develop curriculum content; with businesses and local nonprofits to generate real work assignments; with professionals to help critique student work; with elderly citizens as learning partners; and with other students within the school and across the nation to collaborate on science, history, and English assignments.

Crafting a common vision is one of the most critical stages in the development of curriculum innovations. But it is also perhaps the safest stage; implementing the vision is quite another task. A new set of skills is required if teachers themselves are to help prepare students to live and work in the twenty-first century. Teachers need time—other than on-the-job-training—to try new ideas, learn to work collaboratively with one another, help define research, determine new assessment strategies, and refine visions based on the experience and wisdom of doing. Leadership and administrative buy-in are important factors. If innovations are to continue and flourish, the environment must support new ideas.

The educators we met in this book constantly looked for ways to revitalize classroom curriculum and promote self-esteem for their students. They often worked against long odds and moved into fearful, uncharted territory. Yet they set no limits or boundaries. In the process, they too were energized. They often served as custodians, grant seekers, and brokers. Through it all, they remained advocates for children and positive change. They are representative of the many educators across this country who evangelize access to learning environments that promote creative application of technology in K–12 curriculum. We can all listen to these teachers and respond in ways that support their vision of "building kingdoms for kids" to better ensure a more enlightened, informed, caring, and educated workforce for the future.

Resource Guide

H ere is a list of resources to help guide you in effective and creative use of technology in the classroom and the home. This is obviously not a complete list of all that is available. Many of these resources will lead you to others that we hope you find useful.

Note that organizations listed below may charge a fee for support and services.

The list contains the following categories:

Grant Information

Publications, Special Reports, and Periodicals

Curriculum Software

Assistive Technology References

User Groups

Internet Web Sites

Organizations

National Information Networks and Clearinghouses

Grant Information

Council on Foundations
1828 K Street, N.W., Suite 300
Washington, DC 20036
(202) 466-5722
The Council on Foundations is a nonprofit organization concerned about global issues in our communities. It provides technical support and professional development services to funders. As a service to both grantmakers and grant seekers, the council has established a web site for philanthropic organizations. Visit the council's home page at http://www.cof.org to obtain information on current funding priorities for corporations and private funders.

Education Funding News
(800) 876-0226
This weekly publication provides state and local education grant seekers with information they need to find federal, corporate, and foundation funding for their state or local programs. Readers also receive analysis of all regulatory changes issued by the Department of Education and dozens of other federal agencies operating programs to benefit state and local education programs.

Education Grants Alert
(800) 655-5597
This is a weekly publication that gives K–12 grant seekers weekly notice of upcoming grant competitions from the federal government, private foundations, and corporations. The newsletter also features how-to tips on grant seeking.

The Foundation Center
79 Fifth Avenue
New York, NY 10003-3076
(800) 424-9836
http://fdncenter.org
The Foundation Center, an independent nonprofit organization, works to increase public understanding by maintaining a comprehensive and up-to-date database on foundations and corporate giving programs, by producing directories, and by analyzing trends in foundation support of the nonprofit sector. The center provides information free to the public at five Foundation Center libraries and approximately two hundred cooperating libraries across the country.

GrantsNet Project, Division of Grants Policy and Oversight, Department of Health and Human Services.

GrantsNet, an HHS initiative, provides on-line grant resource information to the public. It provides an on-line information reference service accessible through the HHS Gopher and web servers; and an interactive computer-managed mailing-list service where you can subscribe to various lists, grouped according to a specific topic, and share information and dialogue with other members on the list.
Via Internet connection: gopher.os.dhhs.gov at Port 70
Via the Web, HHS home page: http://os.dhhs.gov

1995 Grant Seekers Guide: A Guide to
Federal Program Officers
(800) 655-5597
This guide provides names and phone numbers of program officers managing grant programs at the Education Department, National Endowment for the Arts, National Science Foundation, Energy Department, and Health and Human Services Department. You are invited to contact program officers to gain tips for developing projects and improving proposals.

National Endowment for the Arts (NEA)
1100 Pennsylvania Avenue
Washington, DC 20506
(202) 682-5400
Grants range from $5,000 to $200,000. Contact NEA for specific guidelines.

Polaris Corporation
North Executive Plaza
2320 E. North Street, Suite JJ
Greenville, SC 29607
(800) 368-3775
This organization provides information and direct service to grant seekers. It hosts grantwriting seminars and publishes a grant seeker's directory of K-12 funders.

Publications

Badgett, Tom, and Corey Sandler. *Welcome to the Internet: From Mystery to Master.* New York: MIS Press, 1995. General reference for novices.

Bernhardt, Victoria L. *The School Portfolio: A Comprehensive Framework for School Improvement.* Princeton Junction, NJ: Eye on Education, 1994. This book shows how to develop a school portfolio as an effective means to develop systemic reform. (609) 799-9188.

California Department of Education. *Building the Future: K-12 Network Technology Planning Guide.* Sacramento: California Department of Education, 1994. This comprehensive document was developed by the state department of education in collaboration with leading educational networking experts. It addresses key issues regarding network implementation in schools. (800) 995-4099.

Clark, R. W. *What School Leaders Can Do to Help Change Teacher Education.* Washington, DC: American Association of Colleges for Teacher Education, 1990.

Classroom Connect. Available in both print and electronic formats, this periodical is geared for teachers and students interested in electronic networking. Each issue profiles resources available on the Internet, provides guidance for integrating these materials into the curriculum, and serves as a forum for teachers to exchange information. (800) 638–1639 or http://www.wentworth.com/classroom/crcpub.html.

Ellis, Arthur, and Jeff Fouts. *Research on School Restructuring.* Princeton Junction, NJ: Eye on Education, 1994. This book takes an analytical look at site-based management, cooperative learning, alternative assessment, instructional grouping alternatives, and many other issues. (609) 799-9188.

Gagdon, Eric. *Point and Click on the Internet.* Berkeley, CA.: Peachpit Press. Offers tips on getting the best use out of your time on the Internet.

Goodlad, John I. *Teachers for Our Nation's Schools.* San Francisco: Jossey-Bass, 1990. (Ref. SP 032 960, ERIC Clearinghouse for Teacher Education, One Du Pont Circle N.W., Suite 610, Washington, DC 20036-1186; 202/293-2450).

Gore, Albert, Jr. "The Information Infrastructure and Technology Act." *EDUCOM Review,* Sept.–Oct. 1992.

Kohl, Herbert. *Growing Minds: On Becoming a Teacher.* New York: HarperCollins, 1984. An inspiring and personal account about the author's concern for children and his experiences teaching them to grow through learning.

Krol, Ed. *The Whole Internet User's Guide and Catalog.* Sebastopol, CA: O'Reilly & Associates, 1994. A thorough reference guide with explanations for each of the Internet's functions, designed primarily for novices.

Kurshan, Barbara, and Deneen Frazier. *Internet (and More) for Kids.* Alameda, CA: Sybex, 1994.

Lengel, James G. *Kids, Computers, and Homework: How You and Your Kids Can Make Schoolwork a Learning Adventure.* New York: Random

House, 1995. This book shows how to use word processing, spreadsheets, graphics, animation, and sound to liven up traditional homework assignments, including book reports, writing assignments, and mapping projects. (800) 793-2665.

Levine, M. *Professional Practice Schools: Building a Model.* Washington, DC: American Federation of Teachers, 1988.

Marsh, Merle. *Everything You Need to Know (But Were Afraid to Ask Your Kids) About the Information Highway.* Palo Alto, CA.: Computer Learning Foundation, 1995. This book covers everything: setting up access to the Internet, designing home- or school-based learning activities for kids and families, efficacy and etiquette in surfing the Net, etc.

Murphy, J. "Helping Teachers Prepare for Work in Restructured Schools." *Journal of Teacher Education,* 1990, *41*(4), 50–56. (Ref. SP 520 216, ERIC Clearinghouse).

Pasch, S. H., and M. C. Pugach. "Collaborative Planning for Urban Professional Development Schools." *Contemporary Education,* 1990, *61*(3), 135–143. (Ref. SP 520 134, ERIC Clearinghouse).

Rigden, Diana. *What Business Leaders Can Do to Help Change Teacher Education.* Washington, DC: American Association of Colleges for Teacher Education, 1995.

Rioux, William, and Nancy Berla. *Innovations in Parent and Family Involvement.* Princeton Junction, NJ: Eye on Education, 1993.

Williams, Bard (Ed.). *The Internet for Teachers.* Foster City, CA.: IDG Books, 1995. Written by teachers, this publication has many activities designed for collaborative work for students K–12 and college.

Special Reports

U.S. Office of Technology Assessment. *Telecommunications, Technology, and Native Americans: Opportunities and Challenges.* Washington, DC: U.S. Government Printing Office. This book examines the potential of telecommunications to improve the socioeconomic conditions of Native Americans, American Indians, Alaska Natives, and Native Hawaiians living in remote areas.

U.S. Department of Labor, Secretary's Commission on Achieving Necessary Skills. *What Work Requires of Schools: A SCANS Report for America 2000.* Washington, DC: U.S. Government Printing Office, June 1991.

Periodicals

The following periodicals provide software reviews, insight into teaching and technology trends, success stories, and information on education funding opportunities.

Electronic Learning
Scholastic, Inc.
(800) 325-6149

Learning and Leading with Technology
International Society for Technology in Education (ISTE)
(800) 336-5191

T.H.E. Journal
Technological Horizons in Education
(714) 730-4011

Technology and Learning
Peter J. Li Education Group
(800) 543-4383

Curriculum Software

Apple Computer, Inc.
(800) 825-2145
For titles and ordering information: (800) 825-2145 or www.education.apple.com.
Apple Curriculum Guides address basic skills areas such as science and language arts. Apple Education Solution Guides deal with specialized subjects such as English as a second language and business education.

The guides provide information about the highest-rated educational software packages and give specific examples of schools that have successfully integrated Macintosh computers into their curriculum. Subject areas include adult literacy, K–12 bilingual and ESL, elementary learning, 7–12 mathematics, 7–12 science, K–12 social studies, and K–12 writing.

Educational Software Preview Guide for 1993–94, International Society for Technology in Education (ISTE), 1993. Contact:
Anita Best
Consortium Chair
(503) 346-2400
e-mail: <ISTE@oregon.uoregon.edu>

Intellimation K–12 Macintosh Software and Multimedia catalogue. Available from:
Intellimation
Dept. 2KF
130 Cremona Drive
P.O. Box 1530
Santa Barbara, CA 93116
(800) 346-8355

Laser Learning Technologies catalogue. Available from:
Laser Learning Technologies Inc.
120 Lakeside Avenue, Suite 240
Seattle, WA 98122-6552
(800) 722-3505

Multimedia and Videodisc Compendium. Available from:
Emerging Technology Consultants, Inc.
2819 Hamline Avenue N.
St. Paul, MN 55113
(612) 639-3973

National Geographic Ed-Tech catalogue. Available from:
National Geographic Society
Educational Services
P.O. Box 98018
Washington, DC 20090–8018
(800) 368-2728

Only the Best: Annual Guide to Highest-Rated Education Software/Multimedia for Preschool–Grade 12. Published by:
Association for Supervision and Curriculum Development
1250 North Pitt Street
Alexandria, VA 22314
(703) 549-9110

Teaching, Learning, and Technology: A Planning Guide
This multimedia-based planning kit helps schools organize and execute a strategic plan: technology, staffing, facilities.
Software allows the user to create compelling multimedia presentations to communicate and promote plans.
(800) 800-APPL (2775)

Videodiscovery Educational Videodisc catalogue. Available from:
Videodiscovery, Inc.
1700 Westlake Avenue N., Suite 600
Seattle, WA 98109–3012
(800) 548-3472

Ztek *Educational Multimedia* catalogue. Available from:
Ztek Co.
P.O. Box 1055
Louisville, KY 40201–1055
(800) 247-1603

Assistive Technology References

Assistive technology modifies the computer environment for use by individuals with disabilities. Adaptations range from simple system software adjustments to screen-reading software for a blind user or voice recognition as a way to bypass the keyboard. Other modifications turn the computer into a "text telephone" for hearing-impaired callers or offer large print for a low-vision person.

Individuals with disabilities use assistive technology for the same reasons anyone else might use a computer: to work, research, read, play, study, learn, communicate, get on-line, publish, perform, and play.

Following are resources for assistive technology products.

Adaptive Rehabilitation
Technologies, Inc.
5 Bessom Street, Suite 175
Marblehead, MA 01945
(617) 639–1930

American Printinghouse
for the Blind
P. O. Box 6085
Louisville, KY 40206–0085
(502) 895–2405

Articulate Systems, Inc.
Center
600 West Cummings Park,
Suite 4500
Parsippany, NJ 07054
(617) 935–5656

Alliance for Technology
Access
2173 E. Francisco Blvd.,
Suite L
San Rafael, CA 94901
(415) 455–4575

Apple Computer, Inc.
Worldwide Disability
Solutions
20525 Mariani Avenue,
MS 36AS
Cupertino, CA 95014
(408) 974–7910/TTY
(800) 755–0601
www2.applecom/disability/
welcome.html

AT&T National Special Needs
5 Woodhollow Road,
Room 1119
Woburn, MA 01801
(800) 233–1222

Berkeley Systems
2095 Rose Street
Berkeley, CA 94709
(510) 540-5535

Blazie Engineering
105 E. Jarrettsville Road
Forest Hill, MD 21050
(410) 893-9333

Brøderbund Software
500 Redwood Blvd.
P.O. Box 6121
Novato, CA 94948-6121
(800) 521-6263

Brown Bag Software
2155 S. Bascom Avenue,
Suite 114
Campbell, CA 95008
(408) 559-4545

Closing the Gap
P. O. Box 68
Henderson, MN 56044
(612) 248-3294

Computer Options for the
Exceptional
49 Overlook Road
Poughkeepsie, NY 12603
(914) 452-1850

Don Johnston, Inc.
1000 N. Rand Road, Bldg. 115
Wauconda, IL 60084
(800) 999-4660

Edmark Corporation
P. O. Box 3903
Bellevue, WA 98009-3903
(800) 426-0856

Educational Resources
1550 Executive Drive
Elgin, IL 60123
(800) 624-2926

IBM Special Needs Systems
411 Burnet Road
Internal Zip 9466
Austin, TX 78758
(800) 426-4832 voice
(800) 426-4833 TTY
Access DOS (800) 426-7282

Innocomp
33195 Wagon Wheel Drive
Solon, OH 44139
(216) 248-6206

IntelliTools, Inc.
55 Leveroni Court, Suite 9
Novato, CA 94949
(800) 899-6687

ISCAN
P.O. Box 2076
Cambridge, MA 02238
(617) 868-5353

Laureate Learning Systems
110 E. Spring Street
Winooski, VT 05404
(800) 562-6801

MacWarehouse
P.O. Box 3013
1690 Oak Street
Lakewood, NJ 08701-3013
(800) 255-6227

Special Needs Project
3463 State Street, Suite 282
Barbara, CA 93105
(805) 683-9633

Toys for Special Children
385 Warburton Avenue
Hastings-on-Hudson, NY 10706
(914) 478-0960

WGBH Descriptive
Video Service
125 Western Avenue
Boston, MA 02134
(617) 492-2777 ext. 3490

Kurzweil Applied
Intelligence
411 Waverley Oaks Road
Waltham, MA 02154
(617) 893-5151

LC Technologies, Inc.
4415 Glenn Rose Street
Fairfax, VA 22032
(703) 425-7509

Pugliese, Davey, &
 Associates, Inc.
5 Bessom Street, Suite 175
Marblehead, MA 01945
(617) 639-1930

TAM
Council for Exceptional Santa
Children
1920 Association Drive
Reston, VA 22091-1589
(800) CEC-READ

Trace Center
University of Wisconsin
Room S-151 Waisman Center
1500 Highland Avenue
Madison, WI 53705
(608) 262-6966

User Groups

User Group Connection
2840 Research Park Drive, Suite 100
Soquel, CA 95073
(800) 350-4842

The User Group Connection provides support to special-interest computer clubs that engage in activities from Internet development to training and software review. The User Group Connection publishes a newsletter and sells refurbished computer software and hardware at discounted rates.

To order your User Connection Kit on-line or obtain information about programs: www.UGConnection.Com

To visit the company store: www.UGStore.Com

Internet Web Sites

http://www.info.apple.com.education
Current Apple product information, success stories about technology, disability solutions, and Apple Classroom of Tomorrow research reports are among the many things you'll find at Apple's education web site.

http://web66.coled.umn.edu (otherwise known as the Internet Cookbook)
This web site is great for teachers who want to visit other schools around the country and participate in various activities and projects. The site features an international directory of schools. Maps allow you to meet someone in your own town or in other parts of the world.

http://www.rbs.edu
Visit the Ralph Bunche school and join in the "Great Penny Toss" math experiment, or explore other possibilities with this Internet-savvy school.

http://www.ota.gov/nativea.html

The Office of Technology Assessment developed the Native American Resource Page, available via OTA Online. Other important information about OTA research reports can be obtained via links to this page.

http:www.globe.gov

Launched by Vice President Gore, this project, the Globe Program, seeks to enlist students in measuring environmental phenomena worldwide and then to link them to scientists for data analysis and interpretation.

http://seawifs.gsfc.nasa.gov/Jason.html

The Jason Foundation for Education, formed by explorer Robert Ballard, organizes annual interactive field trips to a volcano in Hawaii, the Galápagos Islands, Mayan ruins, and other locales. On-line data are shared and discussed with scientists. The site also includes software that helps students study island ecology and offers curriculum suggestions and lesson plans that stress multidisciplinary and hands-on activities.

http://wwmcn.org

The education pages of the Medocino Community Network offer excellent and comprehensive lesson plans on how the Internet can be used in teaching a wide range of subjects. Other pages demonstrate how networking activities can become a focal point for economic and community development and support.

Organizations

American Association for the Advancement of Science (AAAS)
1333 "H" Street, N.W.
Washington, DC 20005
(202) 326–6400
AAAS is a nonprofit organization concerned with advancing and supporting K–12 and higher education science and math curricula. The organization also supports community-based learning organizations

throughout the country. They produce a variety of curriculum material and CD-ROM science software.

(800) 351-SLICK (Science Linkages in the Community).

To obtain information and participate in on-line issue forums: http://www.AAAS.org

Association for the Advancement of Computing in Education, P.O. Box 2966
Charlottesville, VA 22902

Association for Educational Communications and Technology
1126 16th Street, N.W.
Washington, DC 20036

Association of Supervision and Curriculum Development
1250 N. Pitt Street
Alexandria, VA 22314-1403

Bolt Beranek and Newman Inc. (BBN)
10 Moulton Street
Cambridge, MA 02138
(617) 873-3776
(800) 765-4441
BBN provides primarily contract research and development in the computer, communications, information, and physical sciences. The organization partners with schools to determine effective use of advanced technologies that promote collaborative work.

Educational Design Studio, Inc.
P.O. Box 608013
Orlando, FL 32860-8013
phone/fax (407) 292-8515
e-mail: <EDStudio@aol.com>
Educational Design Studio, Inc. is a nonprofit corporation designed to help educators disseminate instructional materials created by and for other educators. Its mission is to provide a vehicle for educators to create, develop, direct, produce, replicate, and distribute a variety of educational products and services.

International Society for Technology in Education (ISTE)
University of Oregon
1787 Agate Street
Eugene, OR 97403–9905
http://isteonline.uoregon.edu
Two ISTE Special Interest Groups (SIGs) have listservs. The listserv for telecommunications is at SIGTEL-L@lists.acs.ohio-state.edu. The listserv for educators is at SIGTE-L@nevada.edu.

ISTE is a membership organization for technology-using educators. The organization publishes *Learning and Leading with Technology* (formerly *The Computing Teacher*), the *Journal of Research on Computing in Education,* and the *ISTE Update* newsletter, as well as eight special-interest periodicals and a large selection of educator-developed books and courseware. ISTE provides education, leadership, and a forum for sharing information through its publications, conferences, workshops, and a network of organization affiliates. ISTE also offers educators the benefits of a U.S. national office, special-interest groups, distance education courses, and on-line information services.

Many ISTE resources are available via telecommunications. ISTE Online contains the ISTE guide to resources and services for technology-using educators, educational technology conference information, selections from education newsgroups, copies of major ISTE reports, educational technology news, contacts for ISTE organization affiliates and special-interest groups, and other information. On America Online, ISTE has a forum on technology in education and training within the federal education department's Teachers Information Network. This area, maintained by ISTE's USA national office, features information on educational technology planning, and policy.

Institute for the Transfer of Technology to Education
National School Boards Association
1680 Duke Street
Alexandria, VA 22314
Research and teacher professional development.

Minnesota Educational Computing Corporation (MECC)
3490 Lexington Avenue N.
St. Paul, MN 55126
Software and training support, professional development opportunities.

Society for Applied Learning Technology
50 Culpepper Street
Warrenton, VA 22186
Support for research and technology application for kindergarten through college.

Teachers & Writers Collaborative
5 Union Square West
New York, NY 10003-3306
(212) 691-6590
http://www.twc.org
The Teachers & Writers Collaborative provides professional development opportunities for K-12 schools and districts. The organization operates a writer's residency program that matches individual teachers and schools with professional writers to aid in the development of writing curricula. Teachers & Writers Collaborative produces materials for site-based professional development workshops and is developing a multi-cultural series for African American, Latino, and Italian literature. TWC plans to offer creative writing workshops on-line—for example, engaging students in collaborative poetry writing.

Teaching and Technology Consortium
P.O. Box 382
Whitethorn, CA 95589
(707) 986-7050
This nonprofit organization provides service and support to computer-using educators, particularly in design and implementation of professional development workshops and school restructuring efforts.

National Information Networks and Clearinghouses

The Educational Resources Information Center (ERIC)
A federally funded national information system that provides access to an extensive body of resources. The ERIC Clearinghouse on Information and Technology (ERIC/IT) is one of sixteen ERIC Clearinghouses nationwide that provide a variety of services, products, and resources at all education levels. (800) LET-ERIC.

Eisenhower National Clearinghouse
An information source for K–12 math and science teachers. The organization also provides on-line links of interest to all educators. http://www.enc.org

National Diffusion Network
This organization's mission is to share information about effective programs in schools and districts around the country. Each year it publishes a catalogue of exemplary programs and supports state facilitators and program developers who assist in program implementation across the country. (212) 219–2134 or e-mail: <tivey@inet.ed.gov>

National Parent Information Network (NPIN)
This organization provides information to parents and people who work with them. Among the materials available are articles, a question-answering service, descriptions of innovative programs, and *Parent News,* an electronic report on timely issues related to parenting and child development. (217) 333–2386 or http://ericps.ed.uiuc.edu/npin/npinhome.html

Glossary of Terms

Adobe Premiere   A software product by Adobe Systems for editing videos on a computer.

Agri-Data   An on-line service providing news and reports to those interested in agriculture.

animation   On a computer, the simulation of movement produced by displaying successive images rapidly on the screen.

AppleLink   A commercial on-line service set up by Apple Computer so that people who develop products for Apple computers could have a formal way of talking directly with Apple and each other. AppleLink serves as a source of official Apple information; using it requires custom software provided by Apple.

Apple OneScanner   An Apple hardware product that provides high-speed scanning of text and images into digital form so that they can be stored in a computer.

Apple IIgs   A non-Macintosh Apple computer with a graphical user interface like the one on the Macintosh.

application   A computer program designed to help you perform work on a computer. Some applications focus on one task, such as word processing. Others, called integrated software, include several applications, such as a word processor, a spreadsheet, and a database program.

BASIC   A computer programming language often taught to beginning programmers because it is easy to learn.

boot   To start up. A computer boots by loading a program into memory from an external storage medium such as a disk. Starting up is often accomplished by first loading a small program, which then reads a larger program into memory. The program is said to "pull itself up by its own bootstraps"—hence the verb *bootstrap* or *boot.*

cabling   A collection of wires used to connect devices such as a printer, keyboard, and mouse to a computer.

CD-ROM   An acronym for compact disc read-only memory. A small storage device that holds roughly six hundred times as much data as a standard computer floppy disk and that cannot be erased or written over.

clicking   Pressing and releasing a mouse button. Clicking a mouse button and using a keyboard are common ways of communicating with a computer.

CompuServe   One of the major publicly available on-line dial-up services. CompuServe specializes in making many independent databases of information available to you. For example, you can search through federal census data, trademark and patent applications, hundreds of newspapers and magazines, and scientific, legal, and medical journals from the past decade. It also offers Internet access.

computer-aided design (CAD)   The use of computer technology both to design a product and to illustrate its components using precision drawing. Computer-aided design is used especially in architecture and in electronic, electrical, mechanical, and aeronautical engineering.

computer bulletin board   *See* electronic bulletin board.

computer network   *See* network.

computer simulation   *See* simulation.

computer typesetting Using a computer to perform typesetting operations such as justification and page formatting to make text suitable for printing.

desktop publishing Using a computer and special software to combine text and graphics to create a document that can be printed on either a computer printer or a typesetting machine.

digitize To convert input (such as drawings, print, or sound) into a form the computer can work with and store. The input is represented in a computer by combinations of zeroes and ones. These two numbers are called binary digits.

dot-matrix printer A printer that produces characters made up of dots by using a wire-pin print head. The word *matrix* refers to the rectangular pattern, or grid, in which the dots are displayed.

download To transfer information from a computer network to a personal computer.

EcoNet A computer network for organizations and individuals working for environmental preservation and sustainability. It is run by the Institute for Global Communications.

electronic bulletin board In an on-line service, an information and message-passing center for dial-up users.

electronic conference On-line communication between three or more people, all at different computers.

electronic mail Messages sent from one computer to another. Electronic mail, or e-mail, can be sent and received on local area networks such as in a school, and on larger communications networks such as the Internet.

electronic message A message sent from one computer to another.

ENAN (Educational Native American Network) A network of teachers, students, administrators, and concerned parents who want to improve the education of all Native American children.

encyclopedia on disk An encyclopedia that is contained on a CD-ROM instead of (or in addition to) being printed as a set of books. An advantage of encyclopedias on disk is that you can search for information quickly and easily. Most encyclopedias on disk contain pictures, and some contain movies and sound.

Ethernet   An industry-standard, high-performance network technology that is widely used for linking Macintosh computers and printers.

file   The basic unit of storage that lets a computer distinguish one set of information from another. A file can be a program, a set of data used by a program, or a document you have created.

file server   A network device, usually consisting of a computer and one or more large-capacity disks, on which network users can store files and applications in order to share them.

floppy disk   A disk made of flexible plastic, as opposed to a hard disk, which is made of metal. The term *floppy* originally applied to disks with flexible jackets, such as 5.25-inch disks, which were literally floppy and could easily be bent. With 3.5-inch disks, the disk itself is flexible, but the jacket is made of hard plastic. Both kinds, however, are called *floppy disks*.

gateway   A device that passes information from one network to another. In addition, the gateway converts the information to a form that the second network can accept.

gateway address   The network ID (identification number) of a gateway.

Gopher   An Internet software tool or program that lets you explore the Internet through menus.

hard drive   On a computer, the hard disk where most of the information is stored. This area provides faster access than floppy disks and is capable of storing much more information.

hardware   A computer and any other physical equipment directly involved in performing tasks on a computer or communicating with one.

HyperCard   A software program designed for the Macintosh that lets users organize information like a stack of index cards. A computer document created using HyperCard can contain text, graphical images, and sound.

HyperCard software   The software used to create a HyperCard document.

hypertext   A way of presenting information so that text, images, sounds, and actions are linked in a complex web of associations. These links let you browse related topics, regardless of their presented order.

ImageWriter   A printer manufactured by Apple Computer. This printer, which uses dot-matrix technology, comes in several models. It is often used in classrooms and the home because it is less expensive than a laser printer.

information services   In computer networks, publicly accessed sources of information. Usually these services contain one or more large databases of frequently updated information. The various educational networks and publicly accessed commercial on-line services are all examples of information services.

interface   A hardware link between two systems, or the software link between a computer and a user.

Internet   The worldwide collection of gateways and networks that use the TCP/IP set of protocols. It links networks together so that all kinds of computers can work together and exchange data.

Internet protocol (IP)   A standard created by the computer scientists who created the Internet's predecessor, ARPANET, to solve the problem of linking dissimilar networks. Your computer must be equipped with the Internet protocol to be able to access the Internet.

IP address   An identifying number assigned to your computer for access by the Internet. IP (Internet protocol) addresses may be permanent or dynamic (temporary), depending on the type of on-line service you have chosen to communicate with the Internet.

keyboard   The part of a computer that resembles a typewriter and lets the user communicate with the computer.

KidWorks   A combined word processing and paint computer program produced by Davidson & Associates for primary-level students and other beginning readers; it displays symbolic representations of words. Children use this program to write and illustrate stories.

laser printer   A printer based on the imaging technology used by photocopiers.

LaserWriter   Any of several models of laser printers manufactured by Apple Computer. The LaserWriter is capable of printing sharper images and is faster than an ImageWriter.

Learning Link   An on-line information service.

listserv   A tool for distributing messages to a list of subscribers who have a shared interest in some subject; once a message is sent to the listserv (derived from *list server*), copies are immediately sent to everyone on the list.

local area network (LAN)   A group of computers that are connected by electronic cabling and that share data, software, and storage capabilities. Most school networks are LANs.

LocalTalk   An Apple product providing a simple network that can connect up to thirty-two Apple computers and printers by using cables that connect to built-in ports on the machines.

LocalTalk configuration   The way LocalTalk's network is laid out, that is, the way its elements are connected.

log on   In a communications session, to connect to the service by identifying yourself.

Macintosh   A family of computers developed by Apple. Older versions include the Macintosh LC II, Macintosh SE, and Macintosh IIci. More recent versions include those in the Power Macintosh and Macintosh Performa categories.

MacroMind Director   A software product by Macromedia, MacroMind Director is used to create desktop video and multimedia presentations.

MacTCP   An Apple product that lets Macintosh computers exchange information with non-Macintosh computers and with other Internet hosts.

modem   An electronic device that links your computer to the on-line world through a telephone line. A modem turns data from your computer into information that can be sent over telephone lines or inter-computer networks.

multimedia   The integration of sound, text, and video and/or anima-tions in a computer-based presentation.

NativeNet   An electronic community that shares information about lives and cultures of the world's indigenous peoples. Its members com-municate by subscribing to electronic mailing lists.

network   A group of computers connected electronically. A network lets users store, retrieve, and exchange information. Most school net-works are local area networks (LANs) because their circuitry connects computers in one physical area. The Internet is a wide area network (WAN) because its circuitry connects computers in more than one area.

network address   An identifying number assigned to your computer and used by others to send electronic mail to you. Also known as the gateway name.

network database   A collection of data whose records can be related to one another in more than one way. Network databases are less rigidly structured than other types of databases.

networked   Interconnected, or linked, for the exchange of informa-tion.

node   On local area networks, an electronic device that is connected to the network and communicates with other network devices.

on-line service   A service you subscribe to that you then reach by log-ging your computer on through a modem.

password   A unique word used to allow one or more people access to a computer system or its confidential files. In a communications ses-sion, a password is required to allow access to the information service or bulletin board.

PeaceNet   A worldwide electronic on-line site serving organizations and individuals working for positive change in the areas of peace, social and economic justice, human rights, and the struggle against racism.

prompt   A symbol that appears on a computer screen to indicate that the computer is ready for you to respond.

QuickTime   Computer software developed by Apple that makes it possible to play movies on a computer.

QuickTime movie   A series of video images with sound that you can play on any computer in which QuickTime is installed.

router   A device that receives messages that have been sent over a network and then forwards them to their correct destinations. By using routers, it is not necessary for two computers to establish a physical connection before a transmission can take place. Internet-connected local area networks (LANs) require a router and a dedicated line (a phone line used solely for this purpose). This type of connection is twice as fast as the fastest modem. A router is identified by its gateway address.

satellite college course   A course broadcast from a central location to various remote areas such as homes and schools via television systems. It thereby allows students to participate in learning without physically sitting in the classroom where the course is being taught.

scanning   A type of optical technology in which light and dark areas (such as text and pictures) on a sheet of paper are converted into information that can be read by and stored in a computer.

scripting   The process of creating instructions that a computer application can understand and use. Also, the statements (typed commands) and syntax (rules for typing commands) that you use to create this text file using any word processing program or text editor.

server   A computer equipped with software that enables multiple individual users access to shared files and other services.

simulation   With computers, the imitation of a physical process by a computer program that causes a computer to respond to changing conditions as if it were the process or object itself.

software   Computer programs (instructions) that cause hardware (the machines) to do work.

SoundPro Edit   An application for editing and manipulating sounds stored in a computer, produced by Aristo-Soft, Inc.

spreadsheet   A computer program that manipulates data and produces a document arranged in columns and rows. It is usually used for numeric data such as budgets.

telecommunications   A general term for the electronic transmission of information from one place to another.

telecommunications links   The connections between all the devices that make up a network.

UNIX computer   Any computer that contains a UNIX or UNIX-compatible operating system. To access the Internet through a UNIX computer with Internet connectivity, you dial in to its log-in, or "shell," account and communicate with the Internet from it.

Wide Area Information Service (WAIS)   An Internet software tool that allows you to search for information in databases and libraries connected to the Internet.

word processing   The process of entering text and editing it on a computer using an application program that manipulates text.

World Wide Web   A hypertext-based Internet service used for browsing Internet resources, including files that incorporate text, graphics, and sound. Using links, it is easy to access other files on the World Wide Web from the file you are viewing.

Index

Computers: for classroom management, 111; for conflict resolution, 108; in education, xiv-xvii; models of use of, xv, xx-xxi; and school restructuring, xvii-xix; supportive role of, 43–44; as tools, xv-xvii, 5–6, 8–9, 43–44, 124; in vocational education, 83, 85–92. *See also* Technology in classroom

Conflict resolution, 108

Corpus, Keith, 1, 8, 11, 17, 21, 25; on future of Newark Studies, 26–27; and Newark Studies curriculum, 3, 4, 5–6; on team teaching, 18–20

Council on Foundations, 162

Culture: and curriculum, 30, 34, 156–157; and Hypertext Folklife Project, 35–41; in Lakota stories, 132–133, 139–141

Curriculum: computer as supporting, 43–44; and cultural background, 30, 34, 156–157; as focus, 8–9; Myths and Legends, 141–142, 143, 145; writing across, 5–6, 10. *See also* Interdisciplinary curriculum

Curriculum software, 167–169

da Silva, André, 17

Darnell, Darrell, 89

Davis, Jonathan, 48–49

De la Garza, Kathy, 109, 119–120

Deane, Rahshan, 14

Decentralization, xviii

DeCory, Seneca, 134, 145–146, 152

DeLong, Cliff, 151

Desktop publishing, 65–66, 86, 95–96, 114–116; *Newark InDepth,* 2–3, 7, 8, 12–16

Di Pilato, George, 69, 73

Diopoulos, John, 111–112, 119, 125, 127

Diori, Hamidou, 120–123

Dos Palos High School, 77–99; Career Path program, 86;

college-bound students, 79, 96–97; grants, 81, 98–99; library, 83, 93; Spanish-language newspaper, 95–96; vision, 157–158; vocational education, 83, 85–92

Dougherty, Jack, 17, 19; and Newark Studies curriculum, 3, 4–5, 6; on public response, 15–16; on student achievement, 12–13, 23; on team teaching, 18, 26; on writing focus, 8–9, 10

Downloading, 116

Duplantier, Kathleen, 30–31, 32, 33–34, 36, 41; on black culture, 39–40; on extensions of computer use, 45–46; journal of, 38–39, 43; on motivation, 46; on parent support, 49–50; on role of computer, 43–44; role of, 50–51; on whole-language learning, 42–43

Earth Lab project, 106–109, 120

Echevarria, Alex, 13–14

EcoNet, 66

Edgewater (Fla.) High School, 148–150, 157

Education: AIDS, 10–11, 26, 116; multicultural, xii-xiii, 17, 26, 35–41; vocational, 83, 85–92. *See also* Schools

Education Funding News, 162

Education Grants Alert, 162

Education Grants program. *See* Apple Education Grants program

Educational Design Studio, Inc., 175

Educational Resources Information Center (ERIC), 178

Eisenhower National Clearinghouse, 178

Electronic bulletin boards, 66, 122, 123

Electronic mail, 102, 106, 148

ENAN (Educational Native American Network), 149

Ethernet, 120

Family English Literacy Project, 82

Farmer, Ginny, 83, 84, 92

Fast Wolf, Jamie, 139, 143

Foundation Center, The, 163

Frey, Don, 90, 92

Gardner, Howard, 50

Gateway address, 121

Grants: at Dos Palos High School, 81, 98–99; information on, 161–163; at Pine Ridge High School, 142, 143; at South Philadelphia High School, 57, 60, 71, 72, 74

GrantsNet Project, 162–163

Gray, Tom, 130, 138, 139, 148; and computers, 141, 147; as consultant, 150; and Lakota stories, 139–141; on Myths and Legends curriculum, 143, 144

Grow, Carol, 37, 47–48, 50

Guadalupe, Harold, 18, 20, 23

Harris, Corey, 7

Health Academy, at South Philadelphia High School, 60, 66, 68

Hernandez, Anna, 88–89

Hicks, Reginald, 36, 41

Horse, Imogene, 146, 147–148

HyperCard, 122–123; for Hypertext Folklife Project, 32–33, 35, 38; at Pine Ridge High School, 141, 143, 145–146, 150–151, 152; at South Philadelphia High School, 60

HyperCard software, 10, 35

Hypertext Folklife Project, 29–51; and black culture, 39–41; and Choctaw Indian culture, 35–38; community involvement in, 34, 35–38; parent participation with, 48–50; student achievement with, 46–47; student involvement with, 34–35, 43;